A World War II Era German/American Love Story

By

Melvin R. Bielawski

authorHOUSE™
1663 Liberty Drive, Suite 200
Bloomington, Indiana 47403
(800) 839-8640
www.AuthorHouse.com

First published by AuthorHouse 03/03/05

ISBN: 1-4208-1095-2 (e)
ISBN: 1-4208-1093-6 (sc)
ISBN: 1-4208-1094-4 (dj)

Library of Congress Control Number: 2004099362

Printed in the United States of America
Bloomington, Indiana

This book is printed on acid-free paper.

Other books written by Melvin R. Bielawski

The Corner

Secession

P.O.W. Camp 78, Zuffenhausen, Germany

Acknowledgments

The writer is grateful for the editing assistance provided by Col. (retired) Tom Gray. There is no question in the writer's mind that Col. Gray's comments improved the quality of this book immeasurably. Thanks to Col. Gray's detailed review and editorial recommendations that have been incorporated into this book, the writer believes the readers of this true love story will be able to better understand the conditions and challenges facing American/German couples who wanted to marry in the immediate post World War II months and years.

The writer is most grateful to his wife Frances who provided assistance in many aspects of this book. Assisting the author in the identification and spelling of the sites in the Berchtesgaden area and helping in recalling the period of our courtship and the associated challenges we faced in our plans to marry. Above all, the author is thankful to his wife for her answer of "Yes" when he asked her to marry him. He is thankful for the beautiful fifty seven years of marriage and the wonderful life we have shared.

This book is dedicated to all of the German and American couples who weathered the political trials and tribulations in the immediate post World War II era to marry. The documentation requirements, unfriendly attitudes of many Americans and Germans who were against such marriages, and the restrictions imposed by the United States Armed Forces even after such marriages took place were unbelievable. Those German and American couples who pioneered these international unions facilitated by tens of thousands of similar marriages in the years to come, albeit without the numerous restrictions, prejudices, and challenges.

Table of Contents

Introduction

As the author of "P.O.W. Camp 78, Zuffenhausen, Germany", I received many favorable comments relative to the description of the conditions and operations within the American camp for German military and political prisoners of World War II. The book also briefly addressed my meeting and subsequent marriage to my wife, Frances Mary Ponn, a German national who was born and raised in Berchtesgaden, Germany. Such marriages between Americans and Germans were prohibited following the end of hostilities.

After reading "P.O.W. Camp 78", several relatives and friends suggested that I write a book describing in greater detail the backgrounds of both my wife and myself with particular emphasis on the trials and tribulations we faced in order to marry, since at the end of WW II, the United States Army with the obvious approval of Washington, D.C., imposed a non-fraternization policy and a policy banning weddings between Americans and German nationals. This book is in response to the aforementioned recommendations.

I have no doubt that many Americans and Germans who were born years after the end of WW II never knew or learned of the policies of the United States governing the personal relationships between American military personnel and German civilians following the end of hostilities between the two nations in May, 1945.

Near the end of the fighting in Europe and while battles were still in progress in the early days of May, 1945, the United States Army imposed two bans. The non-fraternization and wedding bans between the American military personnel and German nationals. The non-fraternization ban prohibited American military personnel, including American civilians employed by the United States military, from having any friendly and personal contact with German civilians including men, women, and children. When the ban was strictly enforced, any American fraternizing with a German national would be fined and subjected to an official reprimand. There were instances, albeit few in number, where American military personal were cited for befriending children. Of course, these were isolated instances. The ban was primarily intended to keep American military men from associating with German ladies and of course with known German NAZI members.

The non-fraternization ban was difficult to enforce in Germany in 1945. Germany had millions of displaced persons (DP's) living throughout the land.

There were instances when it was impossible for the Military Police (MP's) to determine if the civilian being accompanied by an American was a German or a foreign national, i.e., DP. There were Polish, Russian, Hungarian, Italian, Greek, Bulgarian, and, yes, even South American DP's in Germany. Most DP's were forced labor shipped to Germany to help resolve the manpower shortages due to the war. Some were volunteers who willingly came to Germany of their own volition to take advantage of the

German economy. No doubt some came to Germany at a time when the German military forces were having great battlefield successes. But, for whatever reason, the nation was saturated with foreign nationals including women of all ages. Hence, it was difficult if a G.I. (a term used to identify American military personnel) was fraternizing with a DP or a German National.

The most significant problem confronting the M.P.'s was human nature. The American service men were clean, strong, and obviously deprived of female companionship for months if not for years. Concurrently there were the women, both DP's and German, who were deprived of male companionship for long periods of time. The stress of war was over. Both men and women found time to relax. Human nature came into play. Hundred of thousands of Germans and DP's, men and women, were hired by the American military forces to work in hospitals, kitchens, offices, motor pools, the post exchanges (PX's), military commissaries, laundries, as house maids, and in maintenance capacities. These work conditions brought the Americans and Germans, including the DP's, in close contact on a daily basis. It was no wonder that intimate relationships developed between the males and females, regardless of nationality. Enforcing the non-fraternization ban was impossible. There was no doubt in any person's mind that the intent of the ban was primarily to keep the American military personnel from contact with the Germans and specifically the German women. The ban was a failure.

The wedding ban was more easily enforced by the Army. A small number of marriages that took place between American sevicemen and German nationals immediately following the end of hostilities in Germany. The few such marriages that took place in spite of the wedding ban, although illegal, were performed by close friends in the military who had the authority to perform marriages. This was without doubt among friends. Such weddings were not recognized by the State and certainly not by the Army. In order for a marriage to be recognized and considered valid in Germany, it had to be performed by the State. That was the law in 1945 and is still the current law. Not even church weddings were recognized by the State. Most people were initially married by the State and then got married in a church ceremony.

Marriages between American personnel and persons from allies of the United States, for example, England, France, Belgium, Holland, and Luxembourg, had no restrictions. Also not included in the wedding ban were marriages between Americans and displaced persons from such countries as Poland, Russia, Switzerland, and South America. Such marriages numbered in the tens of thousands in the years immediately following the end of WW II.

Both the non-fraternization and wedding bans were lifted by Eisenhower on January 1, 1947. There was little doubt that the bans were lifted primarily for political purposes. Relations between Russia and the United States were beginning to deteriorate rapidly after the end of WW II. The "cold war"

between the Western Powers and Russia was taking center stage. America recognized the need to strengthen the German economy, politically, and, yes, even militarily. There was the danger, either real or perceived, of all of central Europe coming under Communist control. The Russians were in a position to dominate all of Europe if the United States did not take action to thwart the Russian objectives. Improving relations between the United States and Germany became a priority item. Economic aid via the Marshall Plan was extremely significant. Removing barriers between the American military and German civilians was consistent with other actions. Removing the non-fraternization and wedding bans was a significant step in improving relations between the United States and the German people.

Another factor that came into play in the United States decision to remove the bans was pressure from Army Chaplains. There were many American service men who wanted to marry German women. The numbers ranged in the hundreds if not thousands. Army Chaplains were cognizant of the moral issues. They exerted pressures on the American Government to lift the bans.

The action on January 1, 1947, to rescind the wedding ban had several very serious qualifications. The couple who desired to obtain permission to marry would be required to obtain the approval of the marriage by the serviceman's Commanding Officer, a military Chaplain, and, if the American was under twenty one years of age, the approval of a parent or guardian.

In addition, the American would have to have at least six month remaining of his tour in Germany.

The Army would grant the couple, if the marriage was approved by the Army, a seven day "honeymoon" at any Army Recreation Area in Germany. The German national would be required to have a "clean" police report citing the history of the person including information about whether the person was a member of the NAZI Party. The couple would be required to pass physical examinations. All of the documentation would be forwarded to USAEUR HQ (United States Army European Headquarters) for final approval. Upon final approval, the soldier would be required to sign a document indicating that he would never return to Germany. Any American and German couple who were went through all of the procedures required to marry had to be very serious and certainly in love.

This is the story of an American soldier from Toledo, Ohio, who volunteered for immediate induction upon receipt of his first draft notice in May, 1945, and was assigned to Germany later that year where he met a young lady in Berchtesgaden, Germany. The two met, fell in love, overcame the obstacles associated with the non-fraternization and wedding bans, and married. They were fortunate. They traveled together from Berchtesgaden to Toledo, Ohio. Two of their three sons were born in Toledo, Ohio. Mel returned to Germany in July, 1957, with his family. This time in the status of a Department of Army civilian. The cold war between the United States and Russia during the years following the end of WW II resulted in dramatic changes

between the United States and Germany. The pledge Mel signed back in 1947 that he would not return to Germany was null and void. He and Frances had a third son born in Mannheim, Germany, in 1961. Mel and his family returned to the United States in the spring of 1965. He was assigned to the Pentagon in Virginia. The family established roots in Virginia. Mel and Fran, as of this writing, are enjoying retirement in Alexandria, Virginia.

Part I

Chapter One
Germany and World War II

World War I was often referred to as the war to end all wars. Time has repeatedly turned this theory of World War I (WW I) into a fallacy. The world economic and political chaos that followed the end of WW I was, according to some world economists and politicians, one of the leading causes of World War II. The turmoil in the world following the end of WW I encouraged and, to some degree, facilitated the rise to power of national dictators, for example Adolph Hitler, who took advantage of disgruntled populations, poor economies including economic depressions, labor unrest, and a world wide malaise. It would be difficult to identify a period following WW I when peace reigned on earth since the end of the "war to end all wars".

For all practical purposes, all of the would be world powers were involved in attempting to solve their internal economic and political problems following WW I. Most of the nations directly involved in fighting during WW I were concerned with their own post WW I internal affairs. They paid little, if any, attention to world affairs and only when such actions had a direct impact on their own nation. The world paid too little attention to the happenings in Germany and Japan during the 1920's and early 1930's. Concurrently, military actions by Japan in Korea and China went unchecked and Italy was doing its own "thing" in Africa.

The United States, as many nations throughout the world, had very serious internal problems with its economy following WW I. The nation suffered through a colossal economic depression during the 1930's. It had no interest or time to be concerned with what was occurring in Europe, Africa or the Far East. Several key political leaders in Congress advocated total isolationism. They were not concerned with happenings in other parts of the world. The American people were preoccupied with their own problems including mass unemployment, bank failures, and striving to survive from day to day. The United States and the world would pay a terrible price for their short-sighted views and lack of interest in on-going world events.

Germany's aggression in Europe did not initially involve the United States, at least not directly. Adolph Hitler took advantage of Germany's poor economy, the nation's aging political leaders, and the world's lack of attention to assume power and build-up Germany's military forces. Germany re-occupied parts of its former area in neighboring France that were lost after WW I. Hitler also occupied Sudetenland, a part of Chechoslovakia, with justification of bringing together German speaking people. Austria was annexed for the same reason. None of the major world powers seriously challenged Hitler on these actions. Hitler signed a non-aggression Pact with Russia to the surprise of England and France. This was all in preparation for Hitler's attack on his next target for conquest, Poland. Germany's attack on Poland in September, 1936, brought France and England into the conflict and thus began WW II. France and England

had mutual defense agreements with Poland. The Polish armies were no match for the German military forces. Soon after the Germans invaded Poland, the Russian armies also attacked Poland. The Polish resistance was short lived. After Germany conquered Poland, it turned its attention to France and England. The German armed forces, its Armies and Air Force, swept through Luxembourg, Holland, Belgium, and France in short order. Denmark and Norway were occupied by the German hordes. The German military forces seemed unstoppable.

England would receive the brunt of Germany's bombers following the NAZI occupation of France and the low countries. The United States, although neutral, supplied military supplies and equipment to England and later to Russia. England was able to withstand months and years of aerial onslaughts by the German air force. For whatever reasons, Hitler decided not to attempt an invasion of Britain. Historians and many Germans have cited various reasons for Hitler's decision not to invade England. Some believed that Hitler realized he did not have adequate military resources, namely an invasion capability in the form of ships and landing craft. Others suggested that Hitler was not concerned with over-running England, hoping that England would become an ally when Germany attacked Russia. Still others, including some Germans, thought that Hitler wanted to save his military resources for his planned attack on Russia. The author was advised by at least one former German officer that the German forces were prepared to invade England on at least three different occasions but that the military exercises

were suddenly canceled by Hitler. No doubt this will always remain a mystery.

Germany's invasion of Russia ruptured the non-aggression pact between the two nations. Hitler's hatred for Communism and Russia made full circle. Stalin had disregarded all of the warnings of this coming action not only by his own people but by the Western powers. The Russian armies were totally unprepared for the initial onslaught and advances of the German forces.

Japan attacked Pearl Harbor on December 7, 1941, during peace negotiations in Washington, D.C., resulting in the United States declaring war on Japan. Germany and Italy, allies of Japan, declared war on the United States a few days later. Thus the United States became totally involved in WW II. The major nations consisting of the United States, France, England, and Russia became allies in their war against the powers of Germany, Italy, and Japan.

WW II and associated events would impact the entire globe. Not only would millions of people die and tens of millions of others be maimed and impacted in one form or another, the demographics of the world would be changed dramatically. These changes in demographics would have profound impacts on all of Europe, the Middle and Far East, Africa, and particularly on the United States. Millions of Americans would be relocated for various reasons during and following WW II. The war years would require millions of men and women to travel to various parts of the nation and the world in accordance with their military assignments. Most would be introduced to

new life styles, various cultures, different environments, and in many instances meet their future spouses during their military tours of duty. As a result, many military service personnel would settle in locations other than their former home towns upon returning to civilian life. This mobility of Americans was totally different from the pre-WW II years. The war years also involved the migration of millions of Americans from farms and various regions of the nation to the large industrial cities that were in need of help to produce the weapons of war. The needs of the military in terms of bodies and weapons would produce shortages of labor in the manufacturing of guns, ships, planes, tanks, and other war materials. The impact was apparent in the smallest neighborhoods, in the towns, cities, and States throughout America.

Hitler committed several military blunders, for example, attacking Poland knowing that England and France would go to war over this action, invading Russia while still at war with England and France, declaring war on the United States after Japan attacked the United States, failing to listen to his Army generals in his war with Russia, and attempting to fight WW II on two fronts. The German people would pay a high price for Hitler's aggression and his blunders. Being almost totally dependent on imports for war materials, food, and war time essentials such as oil, the people of Germany would be required to make sacrifices beyond their wildest dreams. Rationing would become a way of life. Everything was rationed including food, clothing, fuel, coal, wood, and all necessary items for personal

hygiene. A barter system, a fore-runner to the immediate post WW II years in Germany, would become essential for survival from day to day. Bread and other food stuffs would become treasured acquisitions. Clothing would be scarce and result in the civilian population having to exchange one piece of clothing for another. For example, shoes could be exchanged for a sweater or coat. This was a period for the German consumer to be extra friendly with any store owner, maintain reliable close friends, and try to cultivate relationships with farmers. This last action was most important. Food was necessary for life and could be used for bartering for other items such as clothing, furniture, medicines, and liquor.

Personal contacts were essential for survival. Even though items were rationed and a person had coupons, there would be times when the supplies were not adequate to fill the needs of the people. Standing in a line for hours to obtain a loaf of bread was not unusual and a person had to hope that the bread supply was not exhausted by the time that person reached the counter. All of these hardships seemed pale in comparison to the losses of German lives, both military and civilian, during WW II.

German casualties, dead and wounded, numbered in the millions during WW II. These numbers could hardly be compared to the tens of millions of deaths of Poles, Jews, Russians, French, British, Americans, and others attributed to Hitler and his armed forces. The German people and the world paid a high price for the actions of Hitler and his henchmen. Not only did Germany lose millions of its citizens but the nation was totally

physically destroyed. Major cities and their infrastructures at the end of WW II were in total ruins. It was almost impossible to find a building standing untouched by the war in cities such as Hamburg, Frankfurt, and Munich. At the end of hostilities in Germany, there was no civil Government functioning. Chaos was the order of the day. Fortunately, the Western powers quickly established order via Military Governments.

The American population fared better than the Germans during WW II. The United States was not as dependent as Germany on imports. The nation had ample natural resources to supply the armed forces as well as the civilian population. Some food items were rationed such as meat, certain canned goods, sugar, lard, and flour. But, there was always an abundance at the stores of all of these items. In some instances the meat markets would not require the stamps to cover the purchases. Ironically many people purchased some items because they were rationed. There was a fear that the supplies would run out. At the end of the war, many Americans had consumer goods that would last for months following the end of rationing.

Items that were relatively scarce on the American economy included cigarettes, automotive parts especially tires, and gasoline. The shortages of cigarettes and all tobacco products were due to the Government's purchases for the armed forces. The same could be said for coffee. The automotive parts shortage was due to the war production efforts. The auto manufacturers converted their assembly lines to military vehicles and pertinent parts. The civilian consumers had to make-do with recapped tires,

old spark plugs, and other salvageable critical parts required to operate their vehicles. The civilian Americans fortunate enough to have a vehicle soon learned how to take advantage of cannibalization procedures to keep their vehicles operating. Visits to "junk" yards in a search for spare parts from wrecks became routine.

The most serious shortage impacting the American car owner was the shortage of gasoline. Although gasoline was rationed due to the needs of the military, if the consumers were frugal and developed good driving habits, they could survive without too much difficulty. However, overall the average American consumer fared much better than even our allies and certainly the Germans, Japanese, and the other axis powers. After the United States and its Western allies landed in Normandy, France, on June 6, 1944, concurrent with the Russian armies advancing across Poland and eventually into Germany, the war in Europe was coming to a conclusion rapidly. Hundreds of thousands of allied and German lives were wasted needlessly due to Hitler's refusal to surrender. The war with Germany ended in May, 1945. The occupation of Germany began. The four major allied powers, France, England, Russia, and the United States, occupied all of Germany and Austria. The assigned areas became known as the "Zones of Occupation".

The United States Zone of Occupation included parts of several States of Germany and a section of Berlin. The Americans occupied Berchtesgaden, Bavaria, where Hitler and several of his henchmen had retreats and where the Americans

and their allies expected Hitler to make his last stand. Hitler also had the Eagle's Nest, the Kehlsteinhaus, on top of the Kehlstein mountain. This was a birthday present to Hitler for his 50th birthday from Martin Borman. The building was used for special meetings and entertaining guests. The structure was referred to as the "Eagle's Nest" prior to the war. The name given to the Eagle's Nest has been erroneously attributed by many people as originating from the Americans.

Concurrent with the end of hostilities in Germany, the United States implemented non-fraternization and marriage bans between American military personnel and Germans, Hungarians, and Bulgarians. These nations constituted the AXIS powers at the end of WW II in Europe. Italy was no longer considered a part of the AXIS alignment in May, 1945. Its status had been changed prior to the end of hostilities.

As stated earlier, the non-fraternization ban was soon disregarded when the Army began employing Germans to work in offices, military post exchanges (PX's), kitchens, motor pools, maintenance of facilities, and dozens of other positions thus relieving the military personnel from doing many relatively menial tasks. The doors were open to fraternization of the Americans with all Germans even with German businesses such as publishers of newspapers, bakeries, breweries and wineries, and a multitude of other organizations which provided services and products required by the United States Army of Occupation. American contacts were also necessary with German local government officials, such as personnel offices. This action was

needed to facilitate recruitment of the German locals employed by the American military forces. Needless to say this opened contact between United States Army personnel, primarily G.I.'s, and German women on a daily basis and encouraged more than a few romances.

The war with Japan ended abruptly in August, 1945, when the United States dropped atomic bombs on Hiroshima and Nagasaki. These actions, although still protested by many people, no doubt saved millions of lives of not only American military personnel but also millions of Japanese military and civilians. An allied invasion of the Japanese homeland would have extended the war in the Pacific and proven costly in human lives to both nations. The Japanese atrocities in Korea and China, e.g., the rape of Nanking in China, and the Japanese sneak attack on Pearl Harbor would never be forgotten. Following the surrender of Japan, the United States also had an occupation Army in Japan.

Germany was the main focus of the United States after WW II. Its central position in Europe and the political ramifications of the slow but steady deterioration of relations between the Western allies and Russia dictated a large Army of occupation consisting of British, French, and United States military forces. The close relationships between the American military personnel and the German civilian population, namely between the American soldiers and German frauleins, was inevitable and would certainly lead to many romances. It was only a matter of time until many such romances became more than just casual

relationships but serious affairs and marriage considerations. The Army's ban on marriages between Americans and Germans precluded such action from taking place. Tens of thousands of American military personnel coupled with the American military dependence on German civilians, particularly German women, for administrative and logistical support would make a farce of the Army's "non-fraternization ban". The "Amis", a short term the German's used for Americans, also gained the reputation for being excellent employers.

And so began a new era in Germany on its road to becoming a democracy. The United States began its role as the Army of Occupation in a peaceful, albeit totally devastated, Germany concurrent with the end of hostilities in Europe in May, 1945. The Status of Forces Agreement between the United States and Germany in early 1950 ended the "occupation" of Germany. The agreement altered the official relationship between the two nations. The United States was no longer considered an occupying power but "guests" of the Germans.

Chapter Two
Berchtesgaden Land

The town of Berchtesgaden, Germany, is located in the southernmost part of Germany. It is at the edge of the Bavarian Alps. The town is situated in a small valley and surrounded by majestic mountains. On a typical clear and sunny day, most visitors are impressed by the outstanding scenery of the town, its buildings, and the beautiful green pastures located throughout the entire area. The meadows give the appearance that they were actually painted green. Tourists to the area from all parts of Germany and from all over the world are impressed with the beauty of the area. God truly created a garden spot in this small corner of the Bavarian Alps. The combination of sunshine and adequate rainfall make the area an outstanding dairy country.

The history of Berchtesgaden goes back several centuries. As the story goes the town was founded by Catholic monks. The monks must have been very impressed with the fresh mountain water, abundance of wild game, and the solitude of the area. Some of Berchtesgaden's buildings and churches are centuries old. But they still retain their beauty and stability. In addition to the beautiful Bavarian Alps that surround the town, the entire area contains many outstanding features including several mountain lakes, salt mines, various small but intriguing gorges, numerous historic Catholic Chapels and countless scenic walking trails that provide panoramic views of the town and countryside. The town has access to Salzburg, Austria, approximately fifteen

miles south. Vienna and other parts of Austria, and Munich, the Capital of Bavaria, are within easy reach of Berchtesgaden.

Berchtesgaden has always been a tourist attraction due to its location and many outstanding natural features. The town's attraction prior to Hitler establishing a residence on the Kehlstein and Obersalzberg area was normal for its location, size, and history. However, Hitler's arrival on the scene changed the town's attraction dramatically. From the time Hitler established residence in Berchtesgaden, the town became a major tourist site. The town achieved an international reputation. Germans flocked to the town to see where Hitler had his home. The tourist business flourished as never before. The many hotels, souvenir shops, restaurants, and other tourist attractions were thriving from the offshoot of this new attraction. The notoriety of the town changed dramatically overnight. The town would continue to attract tourists including American military personnel after WW II. The mountains that surround the town are not high in relation to the American and Canadian Rockies. Certainly the Bavarian Alps in general do not tower to 13,000 or 14,000 feet and even higher as do the Rockies. The beauty of the Alps lies in their compactness and proximity to towns and villages located in the valleys. The Alps have no problems with wild bear or other dangerous animals as do the Rockies. The approaches to many areas of the Bavarian Alps and particularly those parts of the Alps in the area of Berchtesgaden bring people to the base of the mountains. The fact that the European continent has been occupied by humans for thousands of years prior to the Americas

being discovered may account for their cleanliness, manicured appearance, and the fact that they are free from wild and very dangerous animals such as bears and mountain lions. People can walk for miles on various trails without fear of being attacked by wild predators. Preservation of this area has been practiced for centuries. The Alps can be considered domesticated in comparison to the American and Canadian Rockies. The Rockies have wild game, for example bears, wolves, and mountain lions. These animals disappeared from the Alps years ago.

The Alps surrounding Berchtesgaden have hiking trails, camping sites, restaurants, and recreation capabilities including mountain climbing that invite the local citizens and tourists to enjoy throughout the year. In addition to the many scenic trails that pass through the valley practically every mountain has at least one trail that begins in the valley and gradually leads to an upper elevation providing an outstanding overview of the town and surrounding countryside.

One of the many unusual and certainly very welcomed features found by hikers and others wondering through the Alps are the restaurants that are located at or near the trails. The food is wholesome and tasty. It is welcomed by the traveler after spending time on the trail observing the very best of scenery that the Alps can offer. The food and scenery nourish the body and soul, especially when served outside on a terrace that overlooks vast fields of green pastures, deep forests, the surrounding mountains, and the valley below. On a bright sunny day, it is a scene that no amount of money can buy.

The mountains have names that historically go back centuries. Some names have legends, e.g., the Watzmann, the second highest mountain in Germany. Legend has it that the Watzmann is considered to reflect a king, queen, and their five children. The mountain top observed from a distance consists of two high peaks that tower over five smaller peaks thus giving some credence to the legend. The top has some snow year round.

The history of some of the names of the mountains has been lost in time. The principal mountains surrounding the town of Berchtesgaden, in addition to the Watzmann, are the Goll, Brett, Jenner, Untersberg, and to a lesser degree the Gruenstein and Lockstein. No doubt the local citizens would not consider the last two named as mountains. But walking up both there is no doubt the average American would consider the Grunstein and Lockstein as mountains, albeit not the greatest challenge to conquer. I have no doubt that the Grunstein is the most demanding of the two. Walking up the trail to the summit requires a person to be physically in good health and knowledgeable of how to conserve energy in the process. A person can easily identify a novice versus an experienced hiker by observing the pace of individuals. A slow but steady pace is ideal. Conserving energy by not talking is a good method of hiking and reaching the summit without gasping for breath or in the worst case scenario passing out at the summit. Many individuals have learned this lesson the hard way, i.e., via experience. But, it is a lesson worthwhile.

The mountain lakes are breath-taking in the area of Berchtesgaden. One of the most famous lakes is Koenigsee. The mountain lake is within walking distance from the center of town. Perhaps four to five miles from the heart of town. It is truly a spectacular lake. The water is pure mountain water, crystal clear, and very cold and deep in the center of the Lake. Swimming in the shallow areas is safe. However, attempting to swim in the center of the Lake is comparable to swimming in a pond of ice cubes. The body becomes tense and the muscles tighten making it virtually impossible to swim. The walk to the Lake from town is scenic and follows the river leading from the edge of the town directly to the Lake. Koenigsee Lake is fed by several mountain streams and waterfalls from the surrounding mountains. At least two of the waterfalls are from the Watzmann mountain.

The water of Koenigsee freezes over in the winter more often than not and provides near perfect conditions for ice skating. The lake is spectacular to tour via tour boats in the summer. The electric powered boats for tourists avoid polluting the waters of the lake. The boats that transport tourists to a Chapel at the far end of the Lake provide an amazing view of the waterfalls and the mountains that surround the Lake. Midway to the Chapel, halfway from shore, the captain of boat may turn off the motor and allow the boat to drift silently as the captain plays a few notes on his trumpet. The echo provides an instant replay for all the tourists in the area, including the people along the shoreline. An outstanding restaurant which serves typical local food and

wild game is also located only a short distance from the Chapel. Included on the menu is trout taken from the Lake. In the winter when the Lake freezes totally, it is possible to walk across the Lake on ice to reach the Chapel and to the smaller lake located just beyond Koenigsee. The deepest spot in Koenigsee is approximately 1000 feet deep. The water temperature even in midsummer is too cold for swimming beyond a few yards from the shore line. In the summer, row boats are available for rental thus permitting a slow, relaxing tour of the entire Lake. On any given summer day, the area is besieged by tourists taking in the beauty of the Lake and the surrounding mountains. The local restaurants have the reputation for serving local, authentic meals with various Bavarian beers.

Hintersee is the second most popular lake in the area and is also noteworthy for its beauty, forests, and mountains surrounding the lake. It is a relatively shallow lake. It can be reached easily from Ramsau, a small village within walking distance of the Hintersee. The walk is very pleasant and passes through one of the most beautiful forests in the Berchtesgaden area. The lake is probably less than a hundred feet at its deepest location. It is ideally suited for tourists on a year round basis. A walk around the entire lake takes less than an hour. Paddle boats are available for children and families in the summer and early fall. It is an ideal way to spend a leisure day on the Lake. The lake normally freezes over in the winter permitting ice skating and a form of ice shuffleboard called curling. The latter is played by the locals, ice conditions permitting. The Hintersee

area has outstanding restaurants that serve favorite local food that more than satisfy the great number of tourists visiting the area annually in all seasons.

Only a short distance from the lake is a National Park that is available to the local citizens and tourists. There are several trails for walking where a family can spend hours viewing the countryside and the mountains bordering the park. The mountains, albeit they are the Alps, have the appearance of the unique Dolomites in Italy in their height and shape. Another interesting feature is the fact that a local farmer has acquired the approval to have his dairy cows roam the Park for feeding on the rich green grass growing throughout the Park's area. The cows meander along minding their own business and pay no attention to the hikers. The ever present cow bells ring loudly throughout the area announcing their presence. Most of the tourists are Germans from the big cities. They take a great interest in the procession of the cows crossing their paths, and feeding on grasses as they plod along. This is a special scene that can only be observed in certain parts of Bavaria. Once witnessed, it can never be forgotten. Another of the many outstanding features of the Berchtesgaden area are the salt mines located within walking distance from the center of the town. This particular feature is typical of many parts of the Alps in Southern Germany as well as in Austria. The salt in the base of the mountains can be traced back to historic periods when that part of the area was covered by the oceans. In fact there is little doubt that the city of Salzburg, Austria, is so named due to

the abundance of the salt mines in the area. It is also noteworthy that the area in Berchtesgaden where the salt mines are located is called Untersalzberg and the area where Hitler had his home was, and still is, referred to as the Obersalzberg. This small but famous area sits below the summit of the Kehlstein on which Hitler had his "tea house" and, as mentioned, was also referred to by the United States military as the "Eagles Nest" when they occupied the town of Berchtesgaden in May, 1945.

There are several small but very scenic gorges located in the area of the town. The one most famous is the Almback Klamm. It is small by comparison to the the many gorges in the United States but unique in its location, i.e., near the town center, and in its compactness. The mountain stream passing through the Klamm is clear and contains many deep pools where a person can observe trout biding their time and waiting for food to come down from the mountain. The Klamm has an outstanding restaurant at its base. There is a miniature mill grinding rough rocks/pebbles into fine almost perfectly round stones. The mill is driven by the water cascading down the gorge.

Berchtesgaden was founded by monks many centuries ago. The religious aspects are visible in the town via the church spires. There are several special chapels in the area that are historical and "must see" on any visitor's itinerary. One of the most interesting and beautiful chapels is "Maria Gern", located a short distance from town and easily accessible via small scenic trails. Walking time may range from thirty minutes to two hours depending on how much time is spent absorbing the various

views of the mountains and the surrounding country side. The driving distance from town to the chapel is only a matter of minutes.

Not only is the Berchtesgaden area free from dangerous wild animals, e.g., mountain lions, bears or other large predators, there are also no rattle snakes or copperheads lurking under leaves or in the forests. It is a safe area for hikers and joggers, at least from these creatures, unlike the many areas in the United States where a person has to be careful and must be constantly aware of the surroundings when hiking or jogging.

The number and variety of walking trails in the area of Berchtesgaden make it ideal for exercising, viewing the mountains, and enjoying the outdoors in the four seasons. The walk to Koenigsee is pleasant. The easy walk around the Hintersee provides a peaceful and scenic view of the lake and its surrounding area. One of the walks that is relatively long but easy on the legs is the trail to the Scharitzkehl area and restaurant. This path provides a spectacular view of the surrounding mountains and particularly of the Watzmann, the lush valleys, an unusual view of Koenigsee, and of the town of Berchtesgaden and the surrounding villages . People can walk up to the Kehlstein via a separate path leading from the same trail if they have the energy. There are many varied walks leading from the town into the mountains, to nearby villages and towns. The number of local restaurants located at or near the end of almost all of the trails in the area entice hikers to quicken their pace as they near their goal. What could be better than sitting down to

a home cooked meal after hours on a scenic trail that made you feel as though you had just seen the very best of nature?

The Berchtegaden area, as almost all of Bavaria, is saturated with Chapels, shrines, and small altars at road sides and at various intersections in the rural areas depicting religious themes. If visitors find that they need some diversity from all of the attractions in the Berchtesgaden area they can make a quick visit to Salzburg, Austria. Historic Salzburg is only minutes away from Berchtesgaden and can easily be reached via public transportation. One of the many attractions in Salzburg is the birthplace of Mozart. The home is located in the old part of the city and is frequented by tourists from all over the world. The city is also famous for its summer music festivals that are generally conducted for several weeks in the July and August time frames.

The Capital of Bavaria, Munich, is also easily accessible from Berchtesgaden via public transportation, i.e., train or bus. The city has various forms of entertainment, such as museums, music festivals, and of course the world famous October Fest that draws visitors from all parts of the world.

All of these features make Berchtesgaden a garden spot. It is truly an outstanding environment to raise a family and certainly provides a quality of life envied by many people who visit the area. The natives are tradition oriented. They have their own unique costumes and very special dress for holidays and special events such as marriages. The people of Berchtesgaden serve special meals found only in the immediate vicinity of the area.

They love the Bavarian Alps and the beautiful setting of the town.

The people enjoy sports such as swimming, hiking, ice skating, skiing and ski jumping. Only ski jumping limits the participation of the Berchtesgaden people to the younger and more hardy men and women in the winter season. Mountain climbing in the late spring through the early fall is similarly limited, albeit not totally, to the younger set. As most Germans, the people enjoy walking. The area is saturated with beautiful paths that lead into the nearby foothills and forests. It was in this paradise that Frances Mary Ponn (Franziska Maria Ponn) was born and raised.

A scene of Nonntal Street in Berchtesgaden, Germany. The first building on the left, at the bottom of the picture, was the apartment building in which Frances and her mother lived. The building still stands today.

A photo of the Maria Gern Chapel

A photo of the Watzmann and area of Berchtesgaden

The Berchtesgaden area

A scene of the Bavarian Alps and forests in the area

The tunnel leading to an elevator that transports tourists to the Eagle's Nest at the top of the Kehlstein mountain

The Eagle's Nest and a view of the Berchtesgaden Valley below. Tourists normally take a special tour bus to reach the parking lot. From there they take an elevator to the summit. The more hardy tourists can walk from the base of the mountain to the top.

Part II

Chapter Three
The Life of Frances Mary Ponn The Childhood Years

On December 9, 1923, Theresa Ponn gave birth to Frances Mary (Franziska Maria), in Berchtesgaden, Germany. Frances was born in a hotel where her mother was employed on Obersalzberg and only a few yards from where Hitler would eventually build his Bavarian mountain home. Frances was the third child born to her parents. The first two, girls, died soon after being born. Frances was named after her father, Francis. Later, Theresa would give birth to a boy but he would die before reaching two years of age due to malnutrition and a lack of calcium. The condition is known as rickets. This was a period in Germany when the economy was in shambles, inflation was out of control, and prices for food and medicines were beyond the reach of most Germans. Unemployment was exceedingly high. In many areas of the nation, the unemployment rate was beyond 25%. World War I had a great impact on Germany. The reparations levied against Germany after WW I played a significant role in the nation's post war years.

As a young child and prior to attending school, Frances usually played in her back yard. Her parents rented an apartment in the suburbs of Berchtesgaden only minutes away from town. The owner of the apartment had a small farm that contained a few cows and pigs. One of the more memorable events Frances experienced was when a piglet was able to get loose from its pen and chased Frances around the yard. Poor Frances was almost

scared to death. Any person watching this spectacle could not help but laugh at the scene taking place. Frances was running and screaming and the piglet running after her and squealing as though the world was coming to an end. Her mother took after the poor piglet with a broom and chased it back into its pen. She gathered Frances into her arms, cuddling her until the sobbing subsided. Her mom knew that the piglet was probably more frightened than Frances. It was an experience Frances would never forget.

But there were many more pleasant days when Frances could walk through the fields, pick flowers that were not on the restricted list and enjoy the beauty of the Bavarian Alps. All of this would come to an end with her enrollment at the local school. As the locals were fond of saying, all good things must come to an end. Frances enjoyed attending school and meeting new friends. Being the only child, attending school gave her the opportunity to meet and play with other neighborhood children.

The childhood of Frances would, under normal circumstances, be the envy of many young people. The school years were filled with joy, even though it was a one room school house that accommodated as least four grades. There were approximately thirty students in the room all of whom were taught by one teacher. The school years were filled with excitement. The teacher enjoyed taking the children for walks in the area and discussing and explaining the various trees and flowers. Weather permitting, the teacher would take the children for long walks on the nearby paths that led through forests and farm lands

explaining nature's blessings to the children. Frances looked forward to attending school every day. She enjoyed the care of the teacher, the learning process, and the companionship of her fellow students. These were the days she would cherish all of her life. It was a peaceful time in Germany.

As the children grew older, the teacher introduced them to music. Frances enjoyed the choir and the related travel arranged by the teacher to such places as Berlin to sing in various concert halls. To travel on a train to distant places was like a dream. This was her first exposure to life outside of the Berchtesgaden area, the land she loved so much and the mountains she viewed as a wall or fence between the town and the outside world. At home, she could sit in her back yard and look up at the sky and only wonder what world existed beyond the mountains. Berlin was surreal. This was a trip and experience Frances could never have imagined during her many thoughts of the outside world sitting in her garden and viewing the sky and clouds and allowing her imagination to run wild. She was intrigued by everything she witnessed during her short but pleasant visit to Berlin. The museums, the mass transportation, and even the dialect of the Berlin natives was very different from the Bavarians, particularly the people in Berchtesgaden. She would have many stories to tell her parents and friends upon returning to Berchtesgaden.

During the visit to Berlin, the students were introduced to television (TV), albeit a screen only about two inches square, a technology that would in the years to come capture the world. Thanks to her music teacher for arranging this very special trip

to what was then the Capital of Germany, Frances' desire to travel was stimulated and would always remain a part of her life. In her youth, she would always dream of someday traveling to various parts of Europe, to South America, and to different parts of the world. These were heavy dreams for a young lady eight years of age. She could never have imagined the travels she would undertake in later years. One of the unusual trips arranged by the teacher was a visit to Hitler's home on Obersalzberg. Hitler, even the demon he was, enjoyed visits from school children. He greeted and shook hands will all of the children. This special trip was more meaningful to the children in the class because of the opportunity to make the long and very beautiful walk from the elementary school which was located in the very heart of Berchtesgaden to Obersalzberg. It was even more meaningful than the chance to shake hands with the Chancellor of Germany. The children, probably like all children at that age, were more interested in getting out of the class room and into nature rather than meeting with politicians. The teacher was the real hero and very much appreciated and loved by the students.

School was always enjoyable for Frances. She especially enjoyed studying geography and data related to the people, customs, and life-styles of foreign lands. She would often sit in her garden and dream about traveling to the various lands she could only view from pictures in her geography books. The nature studies made her more inquisitive and tweaked her interest in science. The field trips conducted by her teachers made her aware of the various unique Alpine flowers. The gymnastics

sessions provided for her physical development and expanded her interests in various sports.

One of her saddest days in school occured when the children were advised that they would be having a new teacher assigned to the class. The teacher whom all of the children worshipped, who took them to Berlin and local appearances to sing at concerts and to many outings to view the surrounding nature in the Berchtesgaden area, was reassigned to another teaching position in a town several miles from Berchtesgaden. The loss of the teacher was a serious emotional blow to the children. They would, however, soon become immersed in their studies with a new teacher but find themselves reminiscing on the excellent lessons learned and interesting experiences with their former teacher. Frances and no doubt many of her classmates would never forget the kindness and warmth of their former teacher.

Frances would spend her school vacations and summer days swimming at the local outdoor natural pool that was located a short bike's ride from her home. She was also kept busy during her school vacations playing with school friends in her neighborhood, picking wild flowers, and reading. While picking wild flowers one day with one of her girl friends in a nearby field, the two were totally engrossed in the task while kneeling in the grass. They became aware of a pair of boots beside them. Looking up they saw a local policeman staring down on them. The policeman told the two young girls the flowers they were picking were under conservation, forbidden to be picked, and proceeded to write a ticket for each of them accordingly. The

fact that they told him they were picking the flowers for their mothers did not deter the policeman from doing his duty. He was intent on enforcing the law. The Germans were very protective of all natural resources including rare flowers such as the Alpine Edelweiss flower that grew only in the mountains. The policeman proceeded to write out the tickets for the two frightened young girls. First, he asked Frances for her name. He then wrote a ticket for this serious act of picking wild flowers under conservation. Then he asked her girl friend to spell her name so that he could also write her ticket. When she completed the spelling and he had written it down on the ticket, he asked her if she was related to the chief of police in Berchtesgaden. Yes, she responded. She was the daughter of the police chief. Even so, he took the flowers from the two girls and kept the tickets as written. Not surprisingly, nothing ever came from the action. No doubt if he turned the tickets over to the chief of police, he could forget about any future promotion. Whether he destroyed the tickets or not was never known. However, this is still typical of the current strict conservation policies of the Germans. They want to maintain their limited resources for future generations to enjoy.

A photo of Frances and her entire class group prior to moving into the town of Berchtesgaden. Frances is the second person from the left in the first row. It was a one room class room and school. The class was comprised of students in the elementary school that included grades 1 through 6.

A photo of Frances on her First Holy Communion day.

In the winter months, weather permitting, Frances would spend many of her weekends ice skating and skiing. In normal Berchtesgaden winter weather conditions, the Koenigsee and Hintersee lakes would freeze over and facilitate the locals enjoying ice skating. This also provided the chance for the more ardent ice skating enthusiasts to practice figure skating. There were several young people who could probably attempt to make the German Olympic team. Unfortunately Bechtesgaden did not have an indoor ice skating facility. Hence, the activity was limited to the cold, wintry days. Frances' ice skating abilities did attract attention on the lake. She was limited to a great extent due to the weather and also the lack of ice skating shoes. Frances, as most children in the town, used ice skates that clamped onto her shoes. Even so, she did excel on the ice. There were a few men and women who offered instructions to the younger people. Their recommendations were always welcomed. In the early spring the ice would begin to thaw making conditions hazardous. The skaters had to limit their skating to the nearby shore lines. There was the hazard of the ice breaking suddenly and thus endangering the lives of the skaters. Falling through the ice into the cold waters of the lake could not be looked upon as a pleasant experience. The potential for drowning or becoming ill with pneumonia was always a threat to the skaters in the later part of the winter season.

The winter months also found hundreds of locals on the ski slopes. The outstanding ski runs in the area also brought many visitors from Munich and other areas of Germany. This was a

time when ski lifts were not in vogue. The skiers carried their skis to the top of the slopes or ski runs. This would often take the better part of the day. The effort was always worthwhile for the thrilling ski run to the valley below that only took a matter of moments. Frances had her own skis that were passed on to her by her father. Weather conditions permitting, the big decision for Frances was to go ice skating or skiing. Both were very enjoyable winter sports and went a long way to making the winters very acceptable no matter how cold or how much snow fell on Berchtesgaden. She would always meet some of her school friends no matter which activity she chose.

Not all things were going brightly during these school years. Her parents divorced while Frances was still a very young girl. The economic depression and runaway inflation in Germany took its toll on many families. Hitler was just coming into power. Frances and her mom moved into the town to make it easier for her mom to walk to work at the local newspaper. She and her mom would live in a small but comfortable apartment only minutes away from the center of Berchtesgaden and in proximity to the new school she would attend. Frances would spend many days meeting and visiting with new girl friends in the neighborhood, yes, still picking flowers, going for short walks, riding her bicycle to the swimming pool, and on occasion sitting in the back yard of the apartment trying to imagine what was on the other side of the mountains. One view that she had was that of the very tip of Hitler's home and also of the Eagle's Nest on top of the Kehlstein. Prior to the WW II, Berchtesgaden

was visited primarily by German tourists, hoping to see where Hitler lived and maybe even obtain a glimpse of the man. Many tourists would stop by Frances' garden and offer a few pennies to her for pointing to Hitler's home on Obersalzberg. The few pennies were enough to buy her a pretzel at the local store.

Frances was approaching her teen years and with that the consideration of a career. Berchtesgaden was and still is to this day dependent on tourism. It is the heart of its economy. Tourism and the salt mines were the main sources of the town's business. There was the possibility of high school. But that would be too expensive for her mother. To send a child to high school would require tuition fees, books, supplies, transportation, and of course extra clothing. Teenagers during that period in Germany either went to a high school or entered a trade as an intern/ apprentice in a field where they could begin their careers as early as thirteen years of age. Frances envisioned herself becoming a beautician. Her grades were excellent and certainly would qualify her and assure success in higher education if her mom could have afforded the expenses. But the family circumstances and finances practically dictated an apprentership in some field of endeavor.

Theresa Ponn, Fran's mother, was employed by the local town's newspaper, The Berchtesgadener Zeitung. The man who owned the paper knew of the family's circumstances and asked Theresa Ponn what career her daughter Frances would be pursuing after her schooling. He asked if he could interview Frances to determine if he could offer her a position with the

newspaper. After the interview and reviewing the grades of Frances, she excelled in working with figures, he offered her a position as an intern working in the accounting area and also in the distribution or sales of the newspaper. Her tasks included collecting circulation and advertising fees. It was an excellent job offer that could not be refused. The beautician career idea quickly went away. Frances began her career in the newspaper business, charting a course in her life that she never even dreamed about during the many hours that she sat in her garden so often wondering what was beyond the scenic mountains. Out of school but still in the learning process, the life of the young girl came to an end and a new window to the future was opened. Frances would spend much of her free time doing what she always enjoyed. Sports in winter and summer kept her busy and also provided diversity to her busy schedules. Frances would have little time and very few opportunities to travel outside of Berchtesgaden. The world outside of Berchtesgaden was a mystery to her but she would still dream of someday exploring the areas beyond the Watzmann and other local mountains, the mountains which seemed to form a wall between the town and the world beyond. Little did she realize that someday she would travel to distant places and areas whose names she did not currently know but would become a part of her daily vocabulary and life. Dramatic changes were about to occur in the life of Frances.

Chapter Four
The Life of Frances Mary Ponn The Teen Years and Internship

It was a totally new experience for Frances when she began her internship with the Berchtesgaden Zeitung, the town's daily newspaper. Beginning her business career while still a teenager had many advantages. She would be starting at the very lowest position in the newspaper office, i.e., performing menial tasks such as typing business letters, assisting in the book-keeping functions, and assisting customers who came into the office to purchase the newspaper. As she gathered experience in the various tasks, especially the book keeping function, the owner of the newspaper began assigning her to other areas including preparing the payroll for all of the employees in the printing shop. Frances was very proud of the fact that she earned her own spending money plus extra pay that she turned over to her mother to help with the household bills. Her mom also had Frances establish a savings account at the bank. This was typical of German frugality and conservatism. With Frances and her mom employed by the newspaper, the two were able to pay the rent, cover daily expenses, and make life more comfortable. They did not live in luxury but were able to survive without any undue hardships. Her mom was able to relax on Sunday afternoons and attend a movie. Frances was able to be active in sports and to meet with her girl friends to take long walks in the area.

The big disadvantage of going to work as a teenager was the fact that her daily life was totally controlled Monday through Saturday noon. This did not cause any serious problems. There were many days when the weather was more conducive to going swimming and taking a long walk to Koenigsee or to Maria Gern as opposed to working in the office. In the winter season, ice skating, skiing, or visiting with one of her close girl friends would be tempting and require her to concentrate on her office duties. But those "other" fun activities would have to wait for Sundays or holidays. Saturday afternoons would be used for shopping, maintaining the apartment, and dealing with other household needs including laundry.

The employment at the newspaper was given priority. After all, this was a career that Frances had never considered. Her personal goal was to become an apprentice hair dresser at one of the local lady's beauty salons. Her school teacher however recognized Frances's special talents with numbers, figures, writing and verbal communications. The teacher spoke to her mother suggesting that if Frances was not going to attend further schooling, she should seek a career in banking or other areas where she could use her special talents. A career in the newspaper business would suit those talents and open doors to a future beyond her dreams. After a relatively short period of time employed by the newspaper, Frances found her work challenging, interesting, and above all very enjoyable. She was thankful to the owner of the newspaper for giving her the opportunity to have employment and a good career.

After a few years of working in the office and assisting the newspaper's female bookkeeper, a new and startling development occured. The lady announced with joy to the owner of the Berchtesgadener Zeitung that she was pregnant and would have to leave the newspaper to have her child. She planned on becoming a full time housewife. She recommended that Frances assume the bookkeeping function. The owner of the newspaper agreed. For the few months prior to leaving her position, the bookkeeper concentrated on training Frances to assume her duties. Everything went as scheduled. Upon the departure of the bookkeeper, Frances assumed her full duties. This new assignment included the responsibility for preparing the payroll for all of the employees. The challenges were enormous for Frances but she attacked her new assignments with gusto. She had tremendous confidence. Several other employees, especially the men, did not appreciate this. A teenager was to hold a principal position on the newspaper staff. But, that was the decision of the owner of the paper and that is the way things would stand. This action was good for Frances. However, the added responsibility would further curtail her extra curricular activities. The time and pressures of her new position would dictate wise use of her free time for relaxing. This would of course limit her activities, including dating.

Prior to September, 1939, with Germany's invasion of Poland and the start of WW II, Frances could enjoy attending the local dances that were very popular. Such dances at nearby cafes and dance halls attracted the German servicemen from

the local Army garrison as well as men from the town who were waiting for their draft calls to enter the military services. If not dancing, accompanied by one or more of her girl friends, she would take long walks on the various trails leading from the town into the foothills of the Alps. With the prospects of war becoming more likely with each passing day, the good times were coming to a close rapidly. With the invasion of Poland and the subsequent German invasion of France and the Netherlands, the public dancing began to decrease. After France and the Benelux countries were occupied, it appeared to the German people that the war years would end. But with the German invasion of Russia, dramatic changes occured in Germany. This was especially true when the reports of casualties began to mount. Public dancing was banned. Such activities were stricly forbidden. The people were more somber. Shortages of food, clothing, and practically all consumer goods appeared overnight. The war came close to home not only in Berchtesgaden but throughout Germany. Daily reports of local men killed in action and the published lists of casualties of the war made the people totally aware of the tragedy of Hitler's regime. These lists coupled with the local military servicemen and women arriving home on convalescent leave due to combat injuries, provided the people of Berchtesgaden with the true developments in the war. Many of these men and women suffered from serious physical and emotional battle scars. All of this information was proof that the news reports that always announced the victories of the German armed forces emanating from Berlin was propaganda. The news coming out of Berlin

was strictly controlled. The really bad news was that it was only the beginning of things to come.

Few Germans realized that the war would last years. However there were many Germans who were very skeptical of the nation's leadership and the direction that they were leading the country. Unfortunately those people were in the minority and were in no position to oppose the Hitler regime. To voice any opposition publicly was an invitation to becoming an inmate at Dachau or other concentration camp established by the NAZI's. Such people were considered political prisoners. Several men from Berchtesgaden spent most of the war years in Dachau due to their anti-Nazi comments.

The local newspaper was controlled by a Government office in Munich. The main topics or news stories were pre-printed and sent to the newspaper for publication. The local paper could not publish any articles about the war, its progress, or data on casualties. It could publish obituaries of local persons killed in action but could not publish any details, for example, where the combat action took place. For the newspaper to print anything else would invite a visit from the local Gestapo Office and, at best, a reprimand. A worst case scenario was the publisher being sent to Dachau and the newspaper closed. The penalties would dissuade any publisher from violating the rules established by the regime.

Every day was different for Frances. New challenges would appear that made life very interesting. One of the most bizarre happenings occured during the early morning hours of one of

her work days. She received a phone call from the local Labor Office indicating that they were sending a French man to her for use in the newspaper as a type setter. She was also advised that he was a French prisoner of war. He was being removed from the camp due to the turmoil he was causing among the other prisoners of war. Apparently he was a confirmed communist and was constantly attempting to convert his fellow prisoners to become believers in communism. This caused constant fights in the camp. Ironically the camp officials decided to remove him from the camp and place him in the local labor market while still being considered a prisoner of war. Frances was told that she would be responsible for securing a place for him to live in Berchtesgaden plus provide him with additional clothing and arrange for him to receive ration stamps for food. Frances was told that the man was a printer in France. The man could barely communicate in German. When the man arrived at the newspaper office, Frances had a difficult time explaining to everyone concerned of the very unusual situation. But, she did have him assigned to the printing shop. She was fortunate in locating a room for him not too distant from the office and near the printing plant. He became the envy of many of the workers. As a prisoner of war, he received packages of food and clothing from the International Red Cross.

He also received rations for food similar to any local German and was even able to purchase new shoes without any problem. This story became more absurd when he applied for leave to return to his home in France and it was granted. Frances and

the other employees were amazed. He promised to return when his leave expired. To believe that this would happen would be naive. The man needed to borrow a coat for his journey home. A local citizen loaned him a coat. The prisoner departed for his "special leave" and, as expected, did not return from his visit home. However, he did return to Berchtesgaden several years after the end of WW II accompanied by his wife. He returned the coat that he had borrowed several years earlier. Yes, strange things did happen. The former prisoner did have a pleasant reunion with some of the men with whom he worked and with the gentleman who loaned him the coat. The wonder of wonders was that after all of those years, he returned the loaned coat to his former benefactor.

Rationing was in effect for almost every item a person could imagine. Bread, meat, clothing, shoes, and any item required for day to day living and for survival was rationed. People could only exchange items, for example, one could advertise a pair of men's or women's shoes for another piece of clothing. People could not advertise to sell or to purchase any items.

The most critical shortage in all of Germany during the war years was food. Hoarding of food was strictly forbidden. The general population had to resort to scavenging for extra food at nearby farms. People stood in line for hours prior to stores opening their doors for business. Word would spread like the plague whenever there was news of an arrival of meat, fruit, or vegetables. Even bread was scarce. Although bread was baked in local bakeries, the flour and ingredients were in very short

supply. The item in abundance in town was salt and that was due to the fact that it was mined locally. Even though the people had ration stamps it did not insure that the food would be available. Every item was precious. On one occasion a line formed to buy the daily publication of the Berchtesgaden Zeitung. A gentleman laid down his loaf of recently purchased bread from a local store to pay for his newspaper. His loaf of bread disappeared. The man cried like a baby. His weekly ration was gone, lost, stolen. As tragic as this event was, there was no way the man could replenish his loss. No doubt, as in every situation where there are shortages of any kind, it pays to have friends who can help. This was a period in time when it certainly was more than helpful to be on friendly terms with the local merchants and nearby farmers. The merchants were a tremendous assist to Frances and her mom. The stores that her mom often frequented prior to and during the war, for example the bakery and meat market, resulted in a close relationship between the store owners and clerks and Fran's mom. The fact that it was a small town and everyone knew each other made life a little more acceptable. The store clerks knew that Frances and her mother were employed by the town's newspaper Monday through Saturday noon. The clerks would not only save the rationed items but set aside "extras" when they did come in to make their purchases. This was a period when food was always in short supply. Frances's mom did all of the cooking to make certain that nothing was wasted. In one sense this was good for the family but Frances was never able to fully learn the secrets of her mother's cooking.

Those were not the times for trial and error in preparing food. Her mother made use of every available ounce of food in the kitchen.

The daily toiletry items such as facial soap, tooth paste and brushes plus bathroom tissue were just not available. People had to make do with what they had on hand. Yes, the daily newspaper had multiple uses besides just containing news, albeit primarily propaganda. It did have a fitting use in the bathrooms. Nothing was wasted.

Frances found some comfort in her walks along various hiking trails into the mountains. Ironically, this is where some of the German soldiers stationed in Berchtesgaden or nearby towns would also find some semblance of peace. The mountains were and always will be a place to relax, find peace of mind, and enjoy nature. Of course, meetings on these outings could only be limited to arranging dates for future walks, swimming, or other sports activities. Dancing or other means of entertainment was out of the question.

The initial victories of the German armed forces, on sea and land, soon were reversed. The Russian armies recouped after several months of terrible losses of men, material, and land. On June 6, 1944, the Western allied armies invaded France. The tide of battle in the Atlantic began to favor the allies. In the interim, the war's casualties and the drain on German manpower resulted in the increased drafting of German females to help the war effort. Women were drafted into the Navy, or Army, to work on farms, and also to work in households where the man of the

family was in service and the wife needed assistance to care for the children.

Suddenly, Frances received a draft notice. It was an alert notifying her that she would soon be required to serve in the German armed forces. She was to report to a duty station in one week. This was a true shock even though it was somewhat expected. She took the draft notice to the lady who managed the newspaper. Since the male owner was drafted, his wife assumed his duties. This was new to her but she had capable people to assist her in keeping the newspaper operational. Frances was, for all practical purposes, the office manager, accountant, book-keeper, payroll clerk, and bill collector. As a result, Frances was an integral part of the business. The lady took action immediately to contact the military authorities to explained the key role Frances played in the operation of the newspaper. Fortunately, she was able to convince the authorities of how important Frances' contribution was and the draft notice was canceled. This was a tremendous relief to Frances and her mother.

Frances had several girl friends who were drafted into the German armed forces. They served in various positions and with different branches of the armed forces. One of her close girl friends was assigned to the German Army operating search lights during allied nightly air raids. Every major city was surrounded by the search lights and also female crews to facilitate the German antiaircraft batteries spotting the allied bombers. This task was critical to the air defenses of the areas under attack. It was also extremely hazardous duty. The lead bombers had

perfect targets as a result of the searchlights. This made crews of the searchlights extremely vulnerable and as a result such duty was almost as bad as being in combat in the front line. The casualty rate among the crews was very high. Concurrently, the lead allied bombers had the unenviable task of being the first in the line of fire. But, in destroying the searchlights, they made the way easier and safer for their buddies who were following close behind only minutes if not seconds away.

German women were also assigned to the navy. Women served in various capacities on ships, for example, in communications, as cooks, and in other functions that were demanding both physically and mentally. These were the unluckiest of the service women. Their lives were more hazardous, the living conditions aboard ship were poor at best. Many were lost at sea due to naval actions. Due to the shortage of manpower, the Germans turned to women to fill their military needs.

At least one of Frances's girl friends was lucky to be drafted to work on a farm. This was like being in paradise considering the food problems on the local economy and the military assignments of females. There was a strong indication that her friend received this plush assignment as a result of the close relationship of her employer and an official in the Office responsible for the assignments of women drafted. In peace and in war, it paid to have good friends. In view of all of the alternatives that Frances was subject to, there was no doubt that her position with the newspaper was a fortunate assignment. It proved again that her employment as an intern years ago was indeed an outstanding

event. Her mother was especially grateful that she could have her daughter near her during those terrible times.

The fact that Frances was past the major hurdle of being exempted from the draft, she could begin to lead a normal life if there was such a thing during the war years. It did mean that she could continue to do her work at the Berchtesganer Zeitung. She would also have week-ends and holidays home and be free to relax and enjoy outdoor outings.

As in most towns located in the Bavarian Alps, many local men enjoyed climbing the mountains on week-ends and holidays. The Berchtesgadener Zeitung had two male printers who were too old to be drafted and perhaps even exempt from the military draft due to their occupation and who enjoyed climbing the mountains on week-ends and holidays. This was good physical exercise and also provided a way to relax. The two men knew Frances enjoyed sports. They invited her to join them one Sunday to climb the Untersberg mountain. This would be a challenge for not only Frances, she had never climbed a mountain previously, but also to the two men. They were aware of the fact that they would have to literally lift and pull Frances foot by foot up the mountain. They started out early one Sunday morning. The weather was perfect. The difficult period was when the they had to scale the "chimney", i.e., climbing between two walls only feet apart. With Frances between them, securely fastened by rope, the men succeeded in scaling the walls and the mountain. Frances felt as though her arms were ready to fall off. But, they had a good view of the valley below and enjoyed their

snacks prior to walking down via an established path. It was an adventure she would always remember.

The newspaper continued publication during the war even while the allied planes flew overhead to various targets in Germany. Many of these flights originated from bases in Italy. There were occasions when the town's air raid sirens would sound and warn the people to go to their bomb shelters located in various parts of Berchtesgaden. The shelters, there were two main ones, were built into the rock of hillsides. They were simple shelters. Nothing elaborate. They could be reached via the street level. The interiors were supported with heavy rafters, had wood floors, and no toilet facilities. The shelters though crude, did serve their purpose. Based on their locations and the nature of the structures, the people inside would be safe unless there was a direct bomb hit. The possibility, though very remote, was always present. The local residents were allowed to take into the shelter one suitcase. This usually consisted of clothing and maybe a few canned goods, if they were fortunate to have such food. The suitcases were permitted to provide the people with some personal possessions in case the town and their homes were bombed. Fortunately the town of Berchtesgaden was never bombed during the war.

Frances kept herself busy. The editor of the newspaper, too old for military service, was a well traveled man. He spoke several languages including Spanish. Frances thought that it would be interesting to learn a foreign language. She took instruction in Spanish from the editor. As the months passed, she was able to

have a limited conversation in Spanish. This was a real delight. Now she was able to joke with her friends that she spoke four languages, German, Bavarian, Austrian, and Spanish.

Frances was invited to visit family friends in Munich in 1944. This was an experience she would never forget. The allied bombers were saturating the German cities night and day. There was no let up. Many times the air raid sirens would alert the people to the coming raids. Many times the alerts turned out to be false. This was due to the bombers attacking other targets that required them to fly over a city such as Munich. As night fell one evening, Frances went to bed feeling secure. No air raid alerts were sounded. However, in the middle of the night the sirens wailed sounding the alarm. This time the target was Munich. It so happened that this was the very worst air raid the city of Munich would experience during the entire war. The family Frances stayed with woke her and led her to the basement of the building. The only good feature was that the home she stayed at was on the outskirts of the city. The center and most of the city was totally destroyed that night. In the morning, Frances and her friends ventured outdoors and witnessed an unbelievable sight. The city was in flames. Fires were evident as far as the eye could see. Her first action was to try to make contact with her mother in Berchtesgaden to advise her that she survived the bombing. It took some time but she finally was able to make a phone call to friends in Berchtesgaden asking them to let her mom know that she was safe and would return to town as soon as possible.

Ironically, with all of the damage to the city and the transportation system, Frances was able to return to Berchtesgaden in a matter of days. One of the many lessons Frances learned from her trip to Munich was the fact that most people living in the suburbs did not trust their cellars or bomb shelters. Many built their own shelters in their back yards. They dug a hole in the ground deep enough to accommodate the family, covered the hole with logs, and than added a few feet of dirt. They believed that only a direct bomb hit would kill them. The ever present danger of a cellar was the possibility of the people drowning if a water pipe burst. This actually happened in some cases. Frances was never again as happy entering Berchtesgaden after her ordeal in Munich. She was home safe and with her mom.

The war was nearing an end in the spring of 1945. The allied armies were in total control of events in Germany. The Russian armies had taken Berlin. The American armies moved rapidly along all its fronts. Air raid sirens continued to be sounded almost every day in Berchtesgaden. Thus far, all of the aircraft flew over to targets beyond the town. Not so on one particular day. On April 25, 1945, the target of the British bombers was Obersalzberg, specifically Hitler's home. The area above the town on the relatively small mountain named Kehlstein. The allies knew exactly where Hitler's Bavarian home was located on Obersalzberg. The bomber pilots also had information of other homes of NAZI leaders that were located on Obersalzberg. The British planes were very exact in dropping their bombs on the

homes of Hitler and his henchmen. Not one bomb was dropped on the town of Berchtesgaden. When the siren alert sounded, Frances was busy at work. She hurried home to join her mom and to hurry into the bomb shelter only fifty meters from her home. However prior to reaching home, the first bombs exploded on Obersalzberg. The concussion lifted Frances a few feet from the ground. But, she and her mom reached the bomb shelter without any further harm. In minutes, it was all over. The people of the town were grateful that the town was spared. They realized that for whatever reason, the town did not suffer the devastating bombing that many German cities and towns had experienced. Soon, the "all clear" sounded. Smoke could be seen rising from Obersalzberg and the area of Hitler's home. It was precision bombing. Life in Berchtesaden would resume. The coming days would bring very interesting and historical events.

It was obvious to most Germans that the war was coming to an end. It could not happen too soon. Every day the war continued would mean the deaths of thousands of military personnel, both among the allies and axis powers. In addition the lives of German civilians, men, women, and children, would be lost due to military action.

Word was received that the allied armies, specifically the Americans, were only hours away from Berchtesgaden. To the people of the town, this was indeed the best news they could receive. The fact that the Americans would be the force to occupy the town was a tremendous relief. The worst fears of all Germans throughout the country was the possibility of the

Russian armies capturing and occupying their cities, towns, and villages. The citizens of the town were uncertain of what to expect. One thing was certain. If the military in the town would decide to resist the approaching Americans, the town would no doubt suffer horrendous casualties. The clock was literally ticking away the hours that would mean the life or death of Berchtesgaden. All of the people in Berchtesgaden would have little rest during the coming nights and days. They were warned to try to have enough food on hand to last several days. No one in the town could forecast the coming events.

The waiting game began. France and her mom had contemplated going to stay with a cousin who lived on Obersalzberg. But they decided against such action. They believed that staying in town was more prudent. Events would prove the decision to be correct. Frances and her mother, in the solitude of their home, wondered what the Americans looked like. After all, neither had seen an American in person except in the movies. Soon their curiosity would be satisfied. And as it would develop, very pleasantly.

Frances in her late teens in a truly typical winter in Berchtesgaden. With snow on the ground, the entire area is a winter wonderland. The Alps appear to have a special luster when covered with a blanket of snow. The air is clear and beckons not only the tourists to Berchtesgaden but also the local citizens to participate in winter sports.

Chapter Five
The American Military Occupation of Berchtesgaden

There was a sense of urgency in the town hall of Berchtesgaden on May 3, 1945. The chief of police, the Mayor, and key public officials had some very serious thinking and talking to do with the Americans only minutes away from the main mountain pass, Halthurm, between Bad Reichenhall and Berchtesgaden. Everyone was cognizant of allied military actions in cities and towns that refused to surrender to the advancing armies peacefully: After given a time limit by the allies to surrender peacefully they would invite the allied Air Forces to bring in their bombers. It was either one or the other. In some instances the decision not to surrender peacefully resulted in saturation bombing, killing thousands of German military and civilians unnecessarily. Yes, the lesson was well learned by the leaders in Berchtesgaden. They decided to send a delegation to the Halthurm Pass to meet the Americans and indicate that there would be no resistance by the German forces. The Mayor advised the local SS and Wermacht leaders of their decision. There were no objections. They all realized it was futile to try to resist. The SS troopers had to worry about saving themselves. Many shed their uniforms in exchange for civilian clothes and took to the woods or went to homes of friends in the town. The Wermacht personnel did the same. They needed no persuasion. The stage was set for the biggest drama in the long history of Berchtesgaden. With assurances from the town's delegation

that there would not be any military resistance in the town, the American troops moved into Berchtesgaden. The date was May 4, 1945. The United States 3rd Infantry Division entered Berchtesgaden without any resistance and to a deserted town center. The people of the town were warned to stay indoors until advised otherwise.

All business activities in Berchtesgaden came to a halt on the day the American military forces marched into town. The Berchtesgadener Zeitung obviously did not plan on publishing any newspaper on May 4 or any time soon. All employees were advised not to report for work and to stay in their homes as the Americans occupied the town. Frances and her mother closed their window shutters, locked the doors, and waited. Later in the day, they looked out the front door to see their first American soldiers standing in the street. This was their first glimpse of what the Americans looked like. To their pleasant surprise, they looked very much like German men, except in different uniforms. The men looked clean shaven, their uniforms were clean, and they each had a colorful scarf around their necks. Frances and her mother became more bold and stuck their heads out of the doorway. One of the Americans approached Frances and, with a map of Berchtesgaden in his hand, asked for directions to a specific building on the street. To the surprise of Frances and her mother, the soldier spoke perfect German. They learned later that his parents migrated to the United States from Germany and they spoke German at home. He indicated that they were looking for a specific building to house a squad of

men for a few days and nights until they would receive orders to move on. The soldier introduced himself as a sergeant and the interpreter for his Commanding Officer. As he spoke to Frances the Commanding Officer, a 1st Lieutenant, approached and said that he wanted to inspect the entire building where Frances and her mom lived. There were several families living in the apartment building. After walking through the building, the Lieutenant said that he and the squad of men with him would move into the building. The interpreter told Frances and her mother that they would have to move out of their apartment, as well as all of the other tenants, to make room for the Lieutenant and his men. Frances told him that there was no place in the town for them or any of the other tenants to move. The town had already been filled with civilian refugees from Munich and other German cities and towns that were destroyed. There was not one spare room in Berchtesgaden or any of the surrounding villages. Frances explained to the interpreter that some of the occupants of the building were invalids. Finally, the Lieutenant agreed that Frances and her mother and the other occupants of the building could remain but they had to give up their bedrooms and that the Army personnel would have access to the kitchens in the various apartments.

This was a tremendous relief to all of the occupants. Frances could us their dining/kitchen area for sleeping. Similar arrangements were made by the Army personnel in the other apartments. As matters developed, this was a blessing for the German occupants. The Lieutenant had a security guard posted

on the outside of the building. This was to protect against marauders, primarily displaced persons, who tried to take advantage of the very chaotic conditions existing in the area, and other renegade allied troops who were guilty of looting and raping local women. The Americans also offered some of their food to Frances and her mother whenever they decided to eat. This too was an outstanding feature which suggested that having the Americans under their roof was worth any minor discomforts. All of the civilian residents of the building were more than satisfied with the American occupation of their apartments for the same reasons. The security of the building in itself was a blessing. The Americans were very generous in sharing their food rations with the civilian occupants of the complex.

On the second day of the troops stay in the apartment, the Lieutenant asked Frances' mother if she would permit her daughter to accompany him to Obersalzberg and Hitler's home. Word was passed around to the American troops that Hitler's home, although bombed and partially destroyed, still had many souvenirs to be had plus the wine cellar was still intact. The Lieutenant was interested in both items. Fran's mother did not give permission for the trip. The Lieutenant returned later in the day with a few souvenir items from his visit to Hitler's home plus several bottles of cognac and wine. The only souvenir consisted of correspondence paper. He distributed the cognac and wine to his troops. It was an interesting "wine tasting" event. The troops would open one bottle at a time. If they did not like the taste they would spit out the wine into buckets. This was an interesting

spectacle witnessed by Fran and her mother. On the third day, the troops departed the building. Fran, her mother, and the occupants were sorry to see them leave. They no longer had their building secured. They would be missing the protection of the American guard. Plus, the troops were extremely considerate in sharing their food rations with the civilian occupants.

The American troops were not gone more than twenty-four hours when there was a knock on the front door of the building. Fran and her mother went together to answer the door. There were several French troops asking if the Americans had left behind any wines and cognac. Obviously, the building was under surveillance while the Americans occupied the apartments. Fran's mom told them that nothing remained except what was in the buckets. The French troops were happy with the contents and departed with the buckets and their contents.

A few days after the Americans moved into Berchtesgaden, the town seemed to be orderly. The streets were very quiet. Fran and her mother decided to venture out to see if any stores were open and to report to their work places at the Berchtesgadener Zeitung. Slowly, the local townspeople began to move out of their homes and venture into the market place in the center of town.

There were still massive troop movements through the town. American, French, and Moroccan troops were passing through to new assignments. It was unnerving for the women who for various reasons had to leave the sanctuary of their homes. The stares of the troops was bone chilling. Word of rapes by some of the allied soldiers made the women leery of being out of their

homes. It became known that some troops would observe the homes or buildings where the women would enter and return at night to search for their prey to perform vicious acts. Such actions were not condoned by the military and the guilty were severely punished or executed if apprehended. However, there was no local police force in the early post-war period throughout Germany. The culprits more often than not were able to evade detection.

Frances returned to work to find that the newspaper office was open and besieged by Americans attempting to obtain printing services. She also learned that the editor of the newspaper was arrested in the first days of the Americans arrival in Bechtesgaden. The Americans took him to the local river across from the main train station. There, underneath a bridge, they interrogated him about his activities during the war. He assured them that he was not a criminal; he had not committed any war crimes; and that he could only publish what the government in Munich sent him. He did ask for the local Catholic priest to vouch for him. After several grueling hours, the editor was released because of the testimony of the priest.

One of the more interesting stories Frances heard happened in early May, just after the Americans moved into Berchtesgaden. The incident took place on her cousin's farm on Obersalzberg. The farm is isolated from the main road. It sits by itself only meters away from a border crossing between Germany and Austria. While the family, comprised of her cousin and her cousin's family were having lunch, American GI came to the door

with his rifle and without further notice entered the home. He walked throughout the living area, not speaking a word, paused in front of the typical Bavarian crucifix in the kitchen area, set his rifle against a table and departed. The family was not only frightened but concerned about the consequences if any other American Army personnel would enter their home only to find an American M-1 rifle but no GI. They stayed in their positions for hours wondering what to do. As suddenly as he disappeared, the soldier returned and entered the home, picked up his rifle and departed. The cousin of Frances could only imagine that the GI had seen the crucifix, figured he was in no danger, took to the woods to sleep. Upon resting for a few hours he decided to go back to town. The cousin mentioned how relieved the entire family was that the soldier did take his M-1 with him.

The wife of the owner of the newspaper, the owner was still on his way home from the war, had to hire an interpreter who spoke English. Frances had been learning to speak Spanish. The paper needed someone to interpret the many requests for printing by the Americans. The interpreter began giving English lessons to Frances. The intepreter was over seventy years old. It was very obvious that the interpreter needed assistance plus he did not want to start a new career. Frances realized that this presented an outstanding opportunity for her to learn a third language. She could never imagine or foresee the impact this action would have on her future. She attacked her studies of the English language as though her life depended on it. Time would prove her endeavor to be more than just worthwhile. Within a

matter of weeks, the gentleman who functioned as the paper's interpreter decided to finally retire. Frances was given the added responsibility of replacing him. This required Frances to use her English language capability daily.

Life in Berchtesgaden changed dramatically with the American occupation. The Americans confiscated most of the hotels in town, including the Post, Bellevue, Deutches House, Berchtesgadener Hof (the most plush hotel in town in May 1945), plus a few others in Bechtesgaden. The American Army also took control of the Platter Hof on Obersalzberg and eventually renamed it the General Walker. Immediately below the Walker was a small guest house that the Americans named the "Skytop". All of these facilities had an American in charge but the entire staffs were local nationals (LN's) hired by the American Army. The Americans referred to the entire complex as the "Bechtesgaden Recreation Area" and made the facilities available to the American troops, American civilians employed by the United States military forces in Europe, and to its allies. Later, with the arrival of dependents of these authorized personnel, the area became known as an excellent family vacation retreat. The famous Chiemsee Lake, located between Munich and Berchtesgaden, was a part of the complex.

The employment of local nationals, including displaced persons (DP's), was beneficial to the American military and the civilians they hired. The military were spared from doing mundane tasks including but not limited to operation of the Army mess halls and kitchen operations, motor pool activities,

laundry operations, post exchange duties, commissary functions, and similar activities. Ironically, Germans who were formerly in the Wermacht and SS and civilian labor forces comprised of DP's were hired to guard military installations. The civilians enjoyed this employment in 1945 and the immediate post-war years not for the pay but for the food they received as a part of their employment agreement. Each civilian employee received one full meal a working day. It was no wonder that many civilians sought to work on week-ends and German holidays to take advantage of the meals. The fact that food was in very short supply on the local economy, provided a special incentive for the civilians to seek employment by the United States armed forces. Obviously the Americans had no shortage of civilians wanting employment. In fact, those selected to be employed by the Americans were the envy of others who were not that fortunate.

The English lessons Frances had taken and her daily use of the language improved her capability to communicate with the Americans coming in for all sorts of printing assistance. She was able to fill a sorely needed gap in the day-to-day business activities between the Americans and the newspaper. This coupled with the return of the male owner of the paper and his excellent knowledge of doing business dramatically improved the paper's response to the American requirements for support. Soon, the majority of the work of the printing plant was in support of the American armed forces. Publication of the Berchtesgaden Zeitung, the town's daily newspaper, was secondary.

The owner recognized that this was also a golden opportunity to obtain food in leu of money, which was practically worthless at the time, for providing printing support to the Americans. The owner explained to the Americans coming to him for support that his employees needed food more than money. The Americans were very agreeable and made certain that ample supplies of food, for example, canned goods, coffee (a luxury item), and even fresh fruit, would be delivered to the newspaper office concurrent with the delivery of printing requirements. Everyone was happy. Close relationships developed between the owner of the paper and the Army clients supported by the printing plant.

Frances usually took the orders from the Americans. More often than not, the Army Chaplain stationed in Berchtesgaden would request church schedules and other routine documents, for example, various church announcements. The needs of the chaplain were recurring. This was good news for Frances and the newspaper. The chaplain was coordinating church services for all denominations with the local Protestant and Catholic clergy. The Chaplain's assistant was a veteran of combat and on a short detail prior to being sent to the States for discharge. He usually provided special goods for distribution to the newspaper's employees.

The American hotels required many types of printing services. Meal menus were required daily and weekly with updates. The workload from this task was enormous. Each hotel managed and operated for the American military personnel would have

separate and distinct menus. They provided support to the locally assigned Army troops and also to the Army personnel who came to Berchesgaden on leave. In addition to the menus, the hotels established a system for paying for drinks and food such as beer. The United States introduced a military scrip in lieu of American currency in Germany immediately after the end of the war. The Army also decided to use a system other than the occupation currency at the recreation centers. Instead of the military scrip currency, a "chit book" was used as cash. The book could be purchased at any hotel desk. One chit, for example, would be worth five cents. A beer might cost ten cents. A book of chits would cost one dollar. All of the chits were printed for the Army by the newspaper. This task was also appreciated by the newspaper for the many returns in food items. As a result of this activity between the Americans and the newspaper, primarily the contact at the newspaper office, Frances became well known by the Americans as the person to see for obtaining printing support. She was the only person in the office who could communicate effectively with the Americans. The owner of the newspaper began to learn enough English to do the business end of the transactions. He turned into a professional negotiator. The employees were more than satisfied with his results especially when he was able to negotiate with the Americans to throw in coffee and cartons of cigarettes with the food. These two items were worth their weight in gold. Not only were they highly desired for personal use but more important they were excellent items for use on the "black market" for bartering purposes for items

of clothing, food, and other consumer goods. Future German generations would not be able to comprehend the economic situation in the immediate years following the end of WW II.

The week-ends, albeit limited to Saturday afternoon and Sunday, provided Frances with an opportunity to relax. Time was set aside for swimming at Koenigsee and a nearby swimming pool. It seemed as though the American arrival occured only a short time ago. The summer weeks passed rapidly. Fall and winter brought few changes to the town. There were still no German tourists visiting the area as they did prior to and during the war. The German civilian population was totally involved in reconstruction efforts. The cities were being rebuilt. The cities and towns had to be cleared of the rubble that resulted from the allied bombings and the ground warfare. The roads and bridges throughout the country either required repairs or total replacing. The destruction and devastation resulting from WW II needed to be addressed as a priority. The infrastructure of all of the major cities in Germany required rebuilding and restoration of services, such as water and natural gas. The challenge of avoiding starvation faced every family in Germany. With all of these problems, the Germans had no time for luxurious travel and vacations. Compounding their problems was the lack of public transportation. Very few Germans had their own motorized vehicles. The German autobahn was void of civilian traffic. If they had bicycles, they were fortunate. It was the main mode of transportation for the majority of Germans. It was a different era. The Germans would be adversely impacted for several years

following the end of WW II. This situation would continue for the foreseeable future. It would take time for the German nation to recover from the devastation that resulted from Hitler's folly. What became more evident in Berchtesgaden in the fall and winter were the great numbers of Americans, including their families, walking in the town center. They were the new tourists, the members of the United States Army of Occupation and their families. The newspaper office was located in the heart of the city, across from the Army billeting office. Frances and her coworkers could observe the Americans at close range. They were intrigued by the clothing of the American women. The relatively bright colors, very fashionable and chic looking.

The Americans were seen every place in town, in local restaurants, at the swimming pool, in the souvenir shops, and even in the clothing stores. In the winter they were on the ski slopes. The Americans even established several ski slopes for beginners in the town and on the Obersalzberg area. It was difficult to distinguish the Americans from the Germans. The three local churches, one Protestant and two Catholic, were attended by the Americans and Germans. It was difficult to imagine that a war could have existed between these two peoples who had so much in common. There were no animosities, at least not on the surface.

The Army was advertising the Berchtesgaden Recreation Area via AFN (Armed Forces Radio Network), and The Stars and Stripes, the unofficial newspaper of the United States military forces. As a result, Berchtesgaden was thriving from

the business. The local restaurants, gift stores and souvenir shops were doing a very good business. There was one minor disadvantage to the local sports fans. The ski slopes and other sport areas were usually saturated with Americans. In the winter, the local slopes were too crowded. The Americans frequented the German restaurants in town. Many of the local businessmen enjoyed the free spending Americans.

Spring and summer of 1946 were just around the corner. More surprises would be in store for Frances. The newspaper support to the Army would increase. This would be due to more American military and their families visiting the area. The Commander of the Berchtesgaden Military Post also decided to publish a newspaper for the Americans stationed in the area and for the Americans visiting Berchtesgaden. Frances and the newspaper had their hands full.

During late 1945 and early 1946, many of the town's men and women who were in the German armed forces began to return. Many were wounded and would require medical treatment. Others were suffering from malnutrition and would require special handling and care. These were the survivors. Many of the town's men and women would never make it back home. They were buried in distant lands, most on the Eastern Front and others in all parts of the world. Many were buried at sea.

During the spring of 1946, Frances and one of her girl friends would spend their free time walking one of the many trails in the area. They would also venture to farms located within the immediate vicinity of Berchtesgaden. The cities of Traunstein and Freilasing were not too distant and could be easily reached by public transportation. Visiting the farms would usually result in making the trips worthwhile. They would return home with vegetables such as potatoes and, if they were really lucky, maybe a chicken or eggs. It was always an adventure. On occasion, the cousin on the farm would deliver bacon, eggs, or other goodies that were in short supply on the local markets. There was little doubt that the various merchants in town did their own business among themselves. The baker would obviously trade with the local butcher or owner of the fruit market and maybe even the shoe maker. No one could really object to these activities. But, they were envied by the average town people who were not in a position to participate.

As summer approached, Frances and any one of her close girl friends would be anxious for the week-ends to go swimming, and even participate in dancing at the local coffee house or cafe. The return of the men and the end of the war brought some semblance of normalcy to the town. On the warm days of summer, especially in July, the time was ripe for visiting Koenigsee to enjoy the luxury of swimming in a cool, crystal clear lake. On July 14, 1946, it would be more than just another day of swimming for Frances. She and one of her girl friends enjoyed the exercise and proceeded to return to Berchtesgaden. However, after walking a short distance, Frances and her girl friend decided to rest on a beautiful grassy knoll overlooking the woods and road that led to town. The events about take place would alter her life beyond her wildest dreams.

Part III

Chapter Six
The Life of Melvin R. Bielawski

Life in Toledo, Ohio

Prior to World War II (WW II), life in Toledo was typical of most American cities. Toledo had very diversified industries that attracted people not only from other parts of the United States but various ethnic groups from all parts of the world, especially from the Central European countries. The immigrants from Germany dominated the numbers, followed closely by families from Poland, Italy, France, and other nations from the area. These relatively large numbers of immigrants made their marks in the latter part of the 19th Century and early 20th Century. More contemporary immigrants represent all parts of the globe from the Americas to Africa, and the Far East.

The glass industry played a key role and Toledo became known as the glass center of the world. The automotive industry, including the manufacture of spare parts, was very strong. Toledo was the rail crossroads between the major cities along the Great Lakes. Railroad traffic moving between Buffalo and Cleveland to Detroit and Chicago and other points west, all traveled through Toledo. Many of the goods were also destined for Toledo. The port operations of Toledo included handling coal, sand for the glass industry, and miscellaneous cargo such as building materials and automotive parts. There were other major employers in Toledo: Toledo Scales, Devilbiss Manufacturing, Houghton Elevators, Bunting Brass, Champion Spark Plug, and

numerous small tool and die making shops dotted the west and south end of the city.

Toledo was not alone in suffering through the economic depression of the 1930's. The entire nation was in economic turmoil. The city of Toledo was hit hard. Unemployment was staggering. Even though the city had diversified industries, every facet of business was adversely impacted by the economic depression. Banks closed overnight. Bankruptcies occured daily. Fortunately the Federal Government instituted the Works Project Administration (WPA) and Civilian Conservation Corps (CCC) to create employment for the masses of unemployed workers. Construction and maintenance of parks, roads, and bridges were the main activities. But it was employment and served the purpose of providing constructive work and income for the unemployed. It was in this environment that Leo and Josephine Bielawski raised their seventh child. Their son, Melvin Robert, was the baby of the family. I had three brothers and four sisters, one of the sisters would pass away as a child. The surviving siblings would treat me as the baby brother throughout their lives. I was always protected from harm in any form. To some extent I was spoiled by the love and consideration the family always thrust upon me. As the youngest member of the family, I was given considerable leeway with my conduct. This despite the fact that I probably deserved to be punished for some indiscretions I had committed as a youth.

My two older brothers established boundaries or limits for all of my outdoor activities including short walks. I was allowed

to venture only fifty yards from the front of our home in either direction. I was told not to pass established markers, for example, a fire hydrant or a telephone pole. The penalty for violating the rules would be tighter restriction on my movements. The fire hydrant, about twenty five yards from home, was like a magnet. The reason in all probability was that an older group of men would usually gather on the front steps of one of the homes just past the fire hydrant to discuss fishing, the weather, activities in the neighborhood, and general gossip. The temptation was just too great on one occasion. I approached the hydrant one day when no one in the group was watching, I placed one foot across the "forbidden" line. I was amazed. Nothing unusual happened. Lightning did not strike me. I was liberated. I accomplished a major move. Before long I was stepping across the ill defined borders and was surprised that no one paid attention to me. New horizons were beginning to open for me.

There were incidents when I did scare my family. On one such occasion I drove my tricycle across a bump on the sidewalk beside our porch. The one thing I remembered was being in the living room and awakening to see one of my sisters bending over me and placing bandages on my chin. It was a terrible looking cut but fortunately more ugly than it really turned out to be. When my parents returned home from work that evening, they were none the wiser. My sister had performed a miracle in covering up my badly cut chin.

There were other serious incidents in my very early life that could have resulted in tragedies. One of my neighbor's sons was

two years older than I. Wherever one of us was found, the other one was nearby. Our association was similar to two brothers. The two of us together were able to get into more mischief than thought humanely possible. On one occasion, Ray and I decided that it would be nice to start a small fire in the middle of the barn located in my back yard. We had a nice fire going in the middle of the barn. Both of us were in the back of the barn admiring our achievement. Very fortunately, my father for some reason or another had to go into the barn.

He was shocked to see what was happening. First, he dashed across the fire and pulled both Ray and I out of the barn and away from the fire. Than he rushed to the outdoor water hose that was already connected for watering the garden and proceeded to extinguish the fire. He was so busy doing this that he did not observe what Ray and I were doing. We were in the neighbor's back yard peering through two knot holes in the five foot high fence watching my father putting out the fire. We did not realize how close we came to being casualties of our innocent, albeit deadly, play.

On another occasion, Ray and I came across a can of liquid tar. Yes, the temptation was just too great to overcome. Ray and I decided it would be nice to wash our hands in the liquid tar. Again, my father came upon the scene. He could not believe his eyes. With a brush, rags, and turpentine, my father had a busy hour cleaning our hands. When it was all over, we were scolded and told in no uncertain terms that we would be in big trouble if we decided to do anything similar in the future.

Of course, there were other instances when Ray and I would do something unusual and cause both of our mothers extra work. Ray had a cousin who lived a block away. The cousin had an old car sitting in the back yard. It was totally inoperable. Ray and I had the bright idea to work on the car. Covered with grease and grime from head to toe, we returned home for dinner. Both mothers almost went into shock. But, they lived through the day with still another memory of their sons and their unpredictable adventures.

I was enrolled in the first grade of Saint Anthony's Catholic elementary school within walking distance of my home. I was in a class with all Polish American students. The class was comprised of an equal number of boys and girls for a total of approximately thirty five students. The group was together for the entire eight years of elementary school with a very few exceptions. Only a very few families ever moved out of the neighborhood. All of the children were either first or second generation Americans. The school's staff consisted entirely of Polish-American Catholic nuns. They were very strict disciplinarians and also excellent teachers. All of the students would soon learn that the nuns meant business and took no nonsense from the students. True, the nuns were intimidating but they were also very patient. The first days of school were difficult for me. The routines alone were a challenge. Every student was required to be in the classroom early in the morning. The day would start with all of the students in the entire eight grades attending a Catholic Mass. After the

Mass, the students would return to their respective classrooms to begin the serious business of studying their lessons.

Melvin on his First Holy Communion day while in the third grade at St. Anthony's Catholic parochial school in Toledo, Ohio. This was a very special day in the Bielawski family. This was the last child of the family.

Both my parents worked to support the family. My introduction to school was welcomed. I did not have the opportunity to attend a "kinder garden" as a preschool pupil. I was starting from scratch. Learning to read and write opened new challenges for a young boy who only kept active playing games at home. I looked forward to each day of school. Homework was a must assignment by the nuns from the early classes until the last day of elementary school. My siblings and parents were happy to see that I not only enjoyed my classes but that I was able to grasp the instructions rapidly. They were very satisfied with the report cards I brought home that identified my progress. It appeared that my lack of a pre-school environment did not adversely impact my capabilities to learn.

As the years progressed, the nuns introduced the students to the history of the United States, geography, arithmetic, English, music, drama, and of course the Polish language. Geography and history captured my interests, more so than any other subjects. I was interested in learning about the United States, Europe, and the other parts of the world. I would try to envision myself traveling to distant places not only within the United States but to foreign lands. I studied maps hours on end of the then forty eight contiguous United States and particularly maps of Central Europe. For outside reading, I enjoyed reading the western novels by Zane Grey. I would read about the American west and life of the cowboys and Indians and hoped that someday I would be able to travel and see the mountains in the West. Toledo is typical of most of the Midwest, that is, relatively flat. I could

not even imagine what a mountain might look like. I looked forward with eager anticipation to attend the matinee movies on Saturdays that were shown at local theaters. Movies such as westerns that contained scenes of the wild west captured my imagination. I would dream of one day traveling not only in the United States but to far off places including Asia and Europe.

I knew that my father was born in a small village named Lawrenzhof in what was than West Prussia. The year was 1878. The town's name was changed to Wawrzynki when the area became a part of Poland in the early 1900's. I also learned that many of my neighbors in Toledo spoke fluent German in addition to Polish. Hopefully, I thought someday I would be able to visit both Poland and Germany. These were just dreams at the age of eleven. Little did I realize during those early years that some of my dreams would be fulfilled in the not too distant future courtesy of the United States Army.

The vacations from school were filled with activities. I enjoyed all sports during the summer vacations. Swimming in local creeks, especially Swan Creek which was one of the better known swimming places. A bathing suit was not required. I also went swimming at a place referred to as "duck pond", so named because it was a pond frequented by ducks and geese in the fall. It was located on the edge of Scott Park, only about two miles walking distance from my home. The big moment arrived when the City of Toledo built a swimming pool at Scott Park. It was the place for swimming. A big disadvantage was the fact that there was absolutely no shade from the sun. More than one

child suffered a severe case of sun burn. But, it was better than swimming in the creek or pond. The more senior boys and girls went swimming in the Maumee River, especially at Walbridge Park, a large amusement park in West Toledo that also had an outstanding zoo and a special dock by the river that was used by the more experienced swimmers in the city.

During the middle grades of elementary school, I organized a softball team comprised of fellow students. The competition was from a team of boys from a neighboring Catholic Parish, St. Stanislaus. It developed into a real rivalry. Considering the ages of all of the boys, they ranged from ten to eleven, it was amazing that we became so competitive. This led to many unusual actions by me and by my team. It was as though we were a part of a major league. I could not wait for the snows of winter to melt to call a practice session in February at Scott Park. Not surprisingly, not all of the team members would appear at the first practice sessions. This did not deter me. If only three boys appeared we would go through batting and fielding practice. There was no harm done. The boys would certainly obtain enough exercise chasing balls hit helter and skelter. But after thirty minutes or so even the hardiest players began to waver and want to go home. But once spring arrived, it was "play ball" time and this the boys did with gusto.

The neighborhood where I lived was dominated by large families. Each family consisted of anywhere from five to ten children. There were boys and girls of all ages ready to participate in various seasonal sports. The warm days of spring, summer,

and fall would lend themselves to fishing, hiking, and playing baseball at Scott Park. The older boys would gather all of the younger boys and march out to Scott Part via back alleys and streets to the various fields available for baseball. Two of the more senior boys, perhaps only four to five years older than the majority of the group, would go through the process of selecting their respective teams, one by one until all of the boys present would be on a team. Every one present at these drafts knew which of the boys were the best players, just like in the major leagues. The best players, and they were known by everyone, would be chosen first. It would follow that the least talented would be the last selected. However, once the game started, it was a new ball game. Reputations meant little. Results of the day were the most important and the game would be dissected inning by inning on the way home from the park.

The winter days were filled with ice skating at Scott Park or sledding and tobogganing at Ottawa Park. The latter Park had a golf course and with it a few hills that facilitated the thrills associated with sledding and tobogganing. The fact that Ottawa Park was more distant from the neighborhood, roughly a distance of approximately four miles, made little difference. After visiting the slopes at Ottawa Park and enjoying the vigorous outdoors for a couple of hours and than walking home, everyone would sleep soundly that night. The winters in the Toledo area were usually cold and the snowfall would usually measure several inches. This provided young boys an opportunity to earn spending money by shoveling snow from the neighborhood sidewalks and store

fronts. It might have been too much snow for the local schools to open but it proved a bonanza for the boys to earn spending money.

I had little time to think about travel but when I did have time it was devoted to wondering if I would ever have the opportunity to travel to distant places like Detroit to see the Detroit Tigers play baseball. Detroit was less than one hour's drive away. I could never imagine having the opportunity to travel to Colorado to see the mountains or to Texas to see real cowboys. The idea of any travel to distant lands was intriguing but didn't seem possible. My school work, activities in the neighborhood, reading, listening with my father to the radio broadcasts of the baseball games of the Detroit Tigers or the Toledo Mud Hens on Sundays followed by the New York Philharmonic Orchestra, were adequate to occupy all of my time.

While still in elementary school and during my teen years, I was influenced a great deal not only by the nuns, my parents and siblings but also by my brothers-in-law. Two of them were very capable of taking care of practically any and all repairs in the home ranging from electrical work to plumbing and carpentry chores. One of the men was a machinist and could also qualify as a tool and die maker. In Toledo, a highly industrial city, a man with these capabilities could almost always find employment and be paid handsomely. The work was very prestigious and satisfying. I believed that it would be a satisfactory way to make a living and a good career.

My brothers and brothers-in-law introduced me to fishing. This I enjoyed.

I was always eager to join in any fishing activities in the Maumee River or better yet in Lake Erie. Fishing for fresh water perch and walleyes was very common on week-ends, holidays, and during vacations. It was an enjoyable sport plus provided the families with excellent dinners. The lakes and rivers were not as polluted as in recent years. From early spring until late fall, the fishing in the Maumee River and Lake Erie waters was outstanding. The winters provided ice fishing on Lake Erie for the more hardy men. A few women enjoyed fishing but they usually did not go ice fishing.

In the later years of attendance at St. Anthony's elementary school, the students began planning for high school. The area where the families lived dictated the high school district and thus the high school the children would attend. Some of the students would attend the Catholic High school if their parents could afford the costs associated with tuition, books, supplies, and transportation. The Catholic High school, Central, was located near the heart of the city of Toledo. It necessitated using public transportation or some other means to travel back and forth to the school. Since in my early years I was interested in becoming a machinist as a trade, I would attend Robinson Jr. High for my first year as a freshman. This was necessary since Macomber Vocational High, located on edge of the business district of downtown Toledo, had grades from the sophomore year through the senior year of high school. Macomber Vocational, as the

name connotes, trained its students for various trades such as automotive mechanics, machinists, office workers, electricians, sheet metalworkers, draftsmen, and numerous other skills. The students attending Macomber normally did not plan on attending college.

My parents and siblings helped me to establish my goals that included the number one priority of obtaining entry to Macomber Vocational High. My attendance at Robinson Jr. High and taking courses in machine shop would prepare me for Macomber. The basic courses in machine shop, as well as other vocational training at Robinson, would be excellent preparatory work for in depth training at Macomber.

Beginning with the German invasion of Poland in September, 1939, and France and England declaring war on Germany due to the treaties between Poland and France and England, the possibility of the United States entering the conflict was addressed by the nuns. One of the nuns, in my seventh grade class, was very prophetic. She told the class that the boys would be in the war. None of the boys could imagine this happening. The conflicts in Europe and the Far East seemed too distant to concern the teenagers as well as their parents. Time would prove the nun's words to be true.

Finally, graduation day arrived in early June, 1941, for the boys and girls of the eight grade of St. Anthony's school. All of the young boys and girls were happy to see the end of a major part of their lives. The eight years were challenging. For some more so than for others. The years were exceedingly important in

building character, confidence, and, perhaps most important of all, obtaining a good, solid education for meeting future demands in life. There was little doubt that attending a parochial school provided the best elementary education obtainable. Now all of the students who were together for eight years were prepared to go on in life to bigger and better things. In retrospect, the eight years went by fast. No doubt many of the boys and girls looked back at those years and reminisced on the more pleasant days of their lives. They were innocent years. Most of the boys would eventually enter the military services. A few would not return. Many would have their lives altered dramatically due to the war and interruptions in the normal lifestyle of the average young man in the neighborhood. The parents of all of the students were proud to see their offspring graduating. My parents and siblings attended the graduation ceremony. It was a very joyous day in the Bielawski household. It was literally the beginning of a new era for the new graduates. Several of the boys and girls who spent eight years in elementary school together, would eventually marry one of their classmates. Many would be separated after scholastic years beginning in the first grade. Some would attend Central Catholic High. Many would attend Scott High also Libbey High, based on where they lived and the school district that dictated the high school they were required to attend. A few, including myself, would attend Robinson Jr. High in preparation for a vocational career.

Chapter Seven
High School Years in Toledo, Ohio

Toledo had many outstanding high schools in 1941. There were several high schools that were excellent in preparing their students for college and also for various employment in other than professional careers. Macomber High, in 1941, was the only male vocational high school in the city of Toledo. However, it had grades from the tenth through the twelfth. Classes in auto mechanics, sheet metal, machine shop, drafting, welding, cabinet making, and office functions were typical courses. Across the street from the all boys school was the equivalent vocational school for girls. It was named Whitney High. The young ladies also had various study options typical at that period for various vocations such as beauty parlor operations and secretarial work.

One can only assume that the vocational schools started at the tenth grade in consideration of the ages of the students. They would have at least one more year as freshman to consider a career path. In my situation the answer was to attend Robinson Jr. High, enroll in machine shop, and then apply for a transfer to Macomber and major in machine shop for the remainder of my high school years. I began attending Robinson Jr. High in September, 1941. This would be an entirely new experience for me. It would expose me to boys and girls other than Polish-Americans. Attending Robinson meant a much longer commute than St. Anthony's. I could not come home for lunch. I took my lunch to school and enjoyed the company of many others in the cafeteria. It was a new and pleasant experience for me. I enjoyed the adventure. I came in contact with students from various ethnic, religious, and racial groups. I enjoyed the new environment, the changes in studies, and the new and diverse young people I met in my classes. The exposure to classes related to science, English at a different level, civics, and especially machine shop were welcomed. The gym classes where I could participate in track, basketball, and other physical activities such as climbing ropes that extended from the gym floor to the ceiling were challenging. These were activities that were totally new to me. If the parochial schools had any shortcomings it would have to be that they offered no organized physical activities.

I developed close friendships with many of the African-American and Jewish boys and girls in my classes. I enjoyed their companionship. It was more remarkable to me that they seemed to enjoy my friendship. It was very unusual to me that there were so many, many surnames that did not end with the typical three letters, i.e., ski. Yes, it was a different world from what I had known. I felt very comfortable in my new environment.

The exposure to the equipment in the machine shop awed me and probably the other young boys. The first few weeks the teacher, who was a qualified machinist, explained the various machines, their functions, the required maintenance, and the potential dangers each was capable of posing if not used properly. I had learned of one of the young men from my neighborhood who had nearly lost his life a few years earlier in the very same

class due to the careless use of a piece of equipment. Fortunately he survived the accident. The teacher also gave a demonstration and explanation of the many precision gauges used for measuring in all machine shop operations. The gauges were based on the metric system. The metric system was explained to the students. This also was new to me and to the majority of students. The teacher was very patient in explaining that the metric system was extremely precise for measuring close tolerances necessary in normal machine shop operations. A knowledge of calipers, micrometers, and other precise measuring gauges would be necessary for anyone entering into careers such as tool and die making, machinists, and even the more skilled machine shop activities. Shop equipment such as lathes, drill presses, shapers, milling machines, and the various hand tools located in any decent machine shop were all available in the school's shop. All of the students would have the opportunity to work with all the equipment before the school year would end. Each of the students would be required to manufacture from scratch a hand tool during the course of the school year.

One major observation I made soon after starting classes at Robinson was that the teachers were much more lenient with the conduct of students in the classrooms. I was amazed that some students would talk during class to fellow students without being reprimanded. This was entirely the opposite of the St. Anthony's class rooms. I was also astonished that there were practically no home work assignments. My parents could not believe that I had no home work when they queried me on the subject. This

was dramatically different from St. Anthony's and the parochial school system of teaching and exercising discipline. The first part of the school year passed rapidly. I was enjoying my new friends and experiences.

The war news occupied the newspapers and radios in the evenings. The war in Europe seemed to monopolize the news. The German armies had control of central Europe. Hitler's forces were fighting the Russians. His air force was bombing England. At the same time, Japan was occupying large areas of the Far East. Korea and China were victims of Japanese aggression. Japan had emissaries in Washington, D.C., discussing peace. It appeared that the United States was avoiding entering the conflict in Europe and, from all indications, also in the Far East.

My friends and I in the neighborhood paid little attention to the activities in Europe and the Far East. These places seemed too remote and distant for many Americans to become overly concerned about. We had company with that type of thinking. In fact, probably the majority of Americans were thinking along the same lines. My friends and I still enjoyed meeting in the evenings and taking long walks as a form of exercise. I also used to entertain my close friends with some of the stories I read in various books. I enjoyed reading. They knew that I had a reservoir of interesting stories to tell, both fiction and non-fiction. I enjoyed telling the stories as much as they enjoyed listening to me. On Sunday evenings we would attend the movies at one of the neighborhood theaters. In early December, we were already discussing the coming Holiday Season and the prospects

of activities in the coming year, 1942. Little did we realize what great changes would come about in the very near future.

On December 7, 1941, several of my friends and I attended a movie at the World theater, so named by the owner. Upon leaving the theater, we were confronted by other friends who were going to attend a later movie. We were told of the Japanese attack on Pearl Harbor, Hawaii. The group had to plead ignorance. No one in the group had ever heard of Pear Harbor. Besides, weren't the Japanese in Washington discussing peace? The answers to these and many more questions that would be raised by more educated Americans would come forth in the days, weeks, and months to come. But one thing these young men did know, the United States was entering the war. This was re-emphasized only days later when Germany and Italy declared war on the United States. The prophesy of the nuns at St. Anthony's elementary school came to pass.

Many of my friends stopped attending school to work in defense factories. They were planning on volunteering for the military forces as soon as they reached seventeen years of age. They could enlist in the armed forces at seventeen years of age providing their parents would give their permission. Many of the boys decided to become employed in the defense industries in the interim. Their plans were short ranged. With so many of the young men volunteering or being drafted into the armed forces, many of the factories were short of labor. The companies did not challenge the ages of the young teenagers applying for work. They were sixteen years of age. As it developed, most of the boys

who were physically fit joined the armed forces as soon as they became seventeen years of age. Unfortunately many of these same boys, who became men in the various military services, returned home after the war with no high school diplomas. They soon discovered that they were at a disadvantage when it came time to compete for jobs. Many would feel the adverse impact throughout their lives. Some of the boys who volunteered at the age of seventeen did not return home. They lost their lives in combat. A few of the boys returned home from the war permanently injured.

I continued to finish my year at Robinson. The moods of the students were more somber after the Christmas break. Everyone was being touched by the war in one form or another. I applied to enter Macomber Vocational High school and was accepted for my sophomore year. I would be entering a new era in my life. The war did not provide for sports and other more normal activities on week-ends. Many of the young men in my neighborhood were off to military training and the war. Of course, those were no longer normal times. The remainder of my year at Robinson Jr. High passed rapidly. The summer of 1942 brought many changes to the lifestyle of all Americans. This was true for me. I did work on a farm not too distant from my home. The activities on week-ends were subdued. Neighborhood men were marching off to war daily. In my spare moments, I would think of the possible impact of the war on my life. I received letters from friends who were in the military. I was intrigued by the places they were assigned and their descriptions of the

various military posts, camps, and stations. Assignments in Texas, Louisiana, Mississippi, Colorado, Wisconsin, Pennsylvania, and so many other locations throughout the United States rekindled my early interest in traveling and also dropping out of school to enlist. But my parents and siblings beat my idea down quickly and emphatically. In a strange sort of way, I envied the men for being in the military and having the opportunity to travel to places that I dreamed of being able to visit. My summer passed rapidly. The next school year was fast approaching. I would experience new and exciting changes.

The fall of 1942 brought with it dramatic developments. Many older boys who reached the age of eighteen and the draft age volunteered immediately for military service. It gave them the opportunity to select their branch of service. Many preferred to be in the Navy or Coast Guard versus the Army. If they were drafted the probability would be an Army assignment.

I began the school year at Macomber eager to learn more about the machine shop functions. It was an interesting schedule. One week was devoted to related classes, for example, drafting, studying business organizations and functions, English, and gym. This schedule provided for an alternate week strictly in a machine shop environment with all of the equipment and tools that would be a part of a functioning commercial machine shop. Macomber was a good four miles from my home. It was excellent to walk providing the weather was acceptable. Taking public transportation was the alternative. I did have a few friends

from the neighborhood for company in my travels to and from school.

The week I attended classes involving how to operate, use, and maintain the machine shop equipment was very challenging. The teacher was a seasoned professional in machine shop operations. The year's agenda called for each student designing and constructing normal household tools such as hammers, various clamps normally referred to as C-clamps, screw drivers, and chisels. In the construction process, the use of lathes, milling machine, drills, and shapers were necessary. In addition, the close tolerances required the use of micrometers and calipers. The use of these machines and tools dictated a need to become familiar with the metric system.

The alternate classroom studies involving drafting taught each student how to design items such as tools. A very important lesson in blueprint reading was learned in the process. Combining the drafting classes with the practical machine shop studies and operations provided a perfect basis for any student to become an apprentice and eventually a qualified machinist or to become employed in any function requiring these two disciplines. The other class room studies included mathematics, such as algebra and trigonometry. These courses and their applications to machine shop operations went hand in hand. Designing tools, machine work, and other similar shop activities demand a knowledge of these subjects. They also broadened the background of the individual and could lead to positions of greater responsibility and promotions.

I especially enjoyed the business classes. The instructor was not only a qualified teacher on the subject but had practical experience in the field of business. Learning the elementary aspects of the various types of business ownerships, the advantages and disadvantages of each, and other functions involved in business captured my attention. Many of my classmates stated that they were bored in this class. It was probably no coincidence that these were the same boys who were eagerly awaiting to enter the military services.

The teacher knew his students. He also recognized that many had no interest in his class and, no doubt he suspected, in any of their other classes. He dwelled extensively on the need for the students to obtain a good education. He was very farsighted in projecting that the war would not last forever and that the students should obtain the best education to prepare themselves for the future. He did take advantage of a day when the weather in Toledo was extremely bad. It was snow mixed with rain, the wind was blowing, and it certainly was not the day to be outdoors, let alone working. At one break in the class the boys all wandered to the window overlooking Monroe Street. There were a dozen men or more working on the street-car tracks. The boys were flabbergasted, speechless. Finally, one of the boys made the comment about the men working outdoors in the terrible weather. Another of the boys stated that it was not fit for a man or beast to be out doors on a day like Toledo was experiencing. Unbeknown to the boys, the instructor was standing behind them wondering what the big attraction was that pulled them to

the window. He obviously heard the comments of the two boys. The instructor took advantage of the situation. He addressed the boys in terms that still ring in my ears, "Take a good look boys. If you don't obtain a good education that is what you will be doing in weather like this after the war".

In the summer of 1943, I was employed by the Willis-Overland Plant in Toledo. I was given the title of "Salvage Inspector". It was a glorified title for a "junk collector". My duties included scavenging the plant for various miscellaneous scrap pipes, iron, and other materials. At the time, the plant's main product was the famous "Jeep" produced for the military. The plant manufactured a variety of other war products including 105mm artillery shells. It was a great opportunity to help in the defense effort and also earn spending money. While performing my various tasks, I had the opportunity to observe the production line for the Jeep. I did not envy the employees. The repetitive functions they performed eight hours a day appeared to be very boring and no doubt tiring.

One major advantage of attending Macomber Vocational High and Whitney Vocational, just across the street from Macomber, was the fact that both schools arranged apprentice training with local industries during the end of the sophomore year. In lieu of spending a week in machine shop in the school, if the student had good grades, the school would arrange for the student who desired to do so to work in a related industry of his selected trade This was a great opportunity to earn money and also learn a trade. I elected to take advantage of this

cooperative plan upon returning to school from the Christmas vacation. I was employed by a local industry in south Toledo. The pay was great. It permitted me to earn spending money and contribute to the welfare of my family. Plus it gave those of us who participated in the program an exposure to the real world. There was one negative aspect of this activity. Most of the work the students were employed at were not apprentice type, i.e., work that would assist in qualifying the boys for full recognition in their various trades. For example, machine shop interns would be primarily employed in production type tasks. These would consist of repetitive type functions performed by machine operators versus highly skilled machinists. This was secondary in the minds of most boys. After all we were providing defense work and preparing ourselves for active military duty. The latter was only a question of time.

The daily news brought home the war and its impact. The newspapers and radios delivered the good and bad news of the war from the far corners of the globe. The war dominated all conversations. My family, friends, and I discussed places addressed in the news that we had never heard of and required looking at maps to pinpoint their locations. North Africa, Sicily, the Islands in the Pacific, all were entering the vocabulary of Americans. The news coupled with letters from family members and friends in the military made everyone aware of the tragedies taking place in Europe, Africa, and the Far East. No day passed without news of new and terrible events caused by the war. It was a very somber period in American history.

Many of my friends quit school as they turned seventeen years of age. The size of the class was half of what it was in the fall of 1943. I was also losing most of my friends in the neighborhood who opted to quit school much earlier and subsequently decided to volunteer for the armed forces. Most volunteered for the Army. Others volunteered for the Navy, Coast Guard, or Marines. I promised my parents that I would wait until I received my first draft call to take my physical to volunteer. One of my closest friends and one of my last buddies in the neighborhood had taken his first physical, passed, and returned home to get his personal life in order prior to reporting for his second and final physical for entering the military. We both had the same reporting date for our physicals, my friend for his second and last call and I for my initial physical. It was possible to volunteer for immediate induction into the armed forces if a person passed the first physical. Since the school year and graduation was less than a month away, plus any student entering the military in the last year of high school would be awarded a high school diploma, I volunteered for immediate induction into the military in order to enter the military service with my friend. On May 22, 1945, I reported for my physical examination in Cleveland, Ohio. The local draft board was very accommodating, they provided the train tickets for all personnel reporting for their physical examinations.

The school photo from Macomber High School in June, 1945.

Chapter Eight
Army Life in the Continental USA

My journey from Toledo to the processing center in Cleveland, Ohio, on May 22, 1945, was only a two hour train ride. It would be several months before I would return home to Toledo, again with the train tickets provided by the United States Government. As expected, I passed the physical examination and was inducted into the Army with several hundred other men from all parts of Ohio. The men who failed to pass the physical examination were considered 4-F, unfit for military service. These men were provided with train or bus tickets for their journey home.

The men who passed the physical examinations were marched to the train station in Cleveland and started their journey into Army life. None of us knew where we were going. After several hours traveling west, the "troop" train pulled into Camp Atterbury, Indiana. This was an interim holding area that gave the Army time to test the mental capabilities of the men and to make military assignments. The men found lacking in reading and writing skills were assigned to "Marblehead", an area of the installation where the men would be tutored prior to being assigned to a military training post, camp, or station.

All the men received the first issues of Army clothing, various immunizations, and an Army indoctrination that included the proper manner to salute officers. The full realization that all of us were in the Army and that a dramatic change in our lives had taken place was when we packaged our civilian clothing for shipment to our homes. This action was sobering.

On the third day, I was given a temporary assignment as a mail clerk. It was also the first opportunity I had to write a letter to my parents. This would be the first of much future correspondence with family and friends from Toledo including friends serving in the military forces in Europe and the Far East.

I enjoyed the new experiences of Army life. Of course, the food was not nearly as good as my mother's home cooking. The Army bunk beds were not as comfortable as my own bed back home. The Army clothing did not fit as well as my civilian clothes. In due time, I would adjust well to these dramatic changes in my life style. I had plenty of company.

In a few days, I and hundreds of other men were told to pack our duffel bags, Army issued bags for clothing, and to report to the local train depot. Each name was called off until all of the men were cleared and told to board the troop train. No one was told the destination of the train. Finally, after one night and part of the following day, the men realized we were traveling south. The final destination was Ft. McClellan, Alabama. We soon learned that the Fort was an infantry training base. The nearest town was Anniston, Alabama. This is where the I would spend the summer months of 1945 together with hundreds of other men. The climate was very different from Toledo located on the western shore of Lake Erie. Toledo has relatively cool summers as compared to Alabama. The heat and high humidity

in Toledo normally occur in late July and early August. It was difficult for me adjusting to the climate, particularly the heat of Anniston, Alabama. All of the troops had to shower at least once a day. I had to wash my fatigues, the duty uniform, every day. The perspiration and the salt from the body dictated the need for this daily chore. The Army issued two sets of fatigues. Of course, I was not alone in this respect. The shower room, large enough to accommodate a dozen men or more, was always totally occupied with men doing the same type of wash. After dinner, the shower room turned into a meeting place for the men. Needless to say it was not something to complain about. The men were not being shot at or engaged in combat in any form. The most serious threats the men faced were the heat and dehydration. The military preached daily to the men to take their salt tablets and to drink plenty of water. This message did not fall on deaf ears. The men who failed to heed this advice suffered the consequences almost immediately. The daily sick call of soldiers was usually due to reactions from the hot, scorching weather of Alabama.

The war with Germany ended in May, 1945. VE-Day (Victory in Europe) ended the hostilities in Europe with the unconditional surrender of Germany. With the end of hostilities in Europe, the emphasis at all American military installations was concentrated on fighting the war in the Pacific Theater of Operations, namely, the Islands of Japan. This would be the nature of the remaining Army training at Ft. McClellan for the next several weeks.

It was fortunate for me that after I was assigned to a barrack area I could call home, I was collocated with other men from Toledo. This was not surprising considering that most of the men reporting to the Cleveland examination center were from Northern Ohio, including the Toledo area. A few of the men were much older and married who were caught in the draft near the end of the war. There was no doubt that their transition from civilian life to a military environment was very much greater than the young and single men. It was this latter group that dominated the number of men in my platoon and Company. We were primarily young men, teenagers, who were drafted into the military services. The training was vigorous. More than a few of the older men could not cope with the physical demands of the training. These men were soon gone from the organization and either discharged or assigned to less physically demanding Army careers. There also were a minor number of men, primarily married and older, who had difficulty making a mental adjustment to the separation from their families and to the rigors of Army life. But these men remained with the organization. They were easily recognized by the other men on Saturday or Sunday evenings when the men could visit the local post exchange (PX) and downed a few beers. These individuals would usually have one too many beers and start reminiscing about their wives and children back home. They would even shed a few tears. The younger men sympathized with these gentlemen. Monday mornings it was back to the old military training routines and the week-end forgotten.

As the summer progressed, the training became more intense. The war in the Pacific theater of operations indicated that the Japanese were defending the various islands to the end. They were fighting to the last man. This was a tragedy in itself. The waste of lives of both the Japanese and allied forces did not make any sense. It proved what indoctrination can do to a soldier. There was little doubt that when the allies, primarily the American armed forces, invaded the Japanese homeland, the action would take the lives of not only millions of Japanese military and civilians but also more than a million lives of American service men and women. It was not a question of whether the military action would require the allied forces to invade Japan but when such an action would be taken. The United States and its allies prepared for the invasion. The military training at Ft. McClellan and the dozens of other military posts, camps, and stations throughout the United States continued in preparation for the forthcoming invasion of Japan. I and my fellow buddies knew that our military training would help us in the final analysis. The training intensified with emphasis on house to house combat. If we were to invade the Japanese home islands, we would be well trained.

There were some hilarious experiences at Ft. McClellan, at least they were entertaining to me. I never bothered to read the Company's bulletin board to learn if I was on any special work details. For example, the Company mess hall was totally staffed with Army personnel. The cooks were a permanent staff consisting of trained personnel in cooking and baking. They

were also augmented daily by the draftees to serve the food, peel potatoes, clean the dining tables, wash dishes, and other menial non-professional tasks. These personnel were to tie a towel at the end of their bunk bed prior to lights out. By taking this action, the CQ or charge of quarters would know exactly which barrack and bunk bed to visit at 4:00 A.M. each and every morning to wake the person(s), to report to the Company's mess hall without waking the entire floor or barrack of men sleeping. Well, I did not know I was on the roster for KP, kitchen police, duty. I never read the bulletin board. One morning all of the lights on the floor went on and the CQ, at the top of his voice, shouted several obscenities at 4 A.M. and asked where Bielawski was sleeping. He further shouted, with more obscenities, that the lights would stay on until Bielawski came forward, dressed, and ready to report for KP duty. I was suddenly thrust upward from my bunk, I had the top bunk, by my buddy (?) below me who kicked me into the air with added obscenities. The entire floor of men, approximately sixty men, suddenly picked up the chorus. That was probably the fastest I moved during the entire training cycle. I was very fortunate. The men did not pay attention to me when I was passing out the "extra" portions of scrambled eggs and bacon to my "room-mates".

In August, 1945, the news that the United States had used the atomic bomb on Japan brought bewilderment to me and my fellow soldiers. There was no doubt that the entire nation, if not the world, experienced the same reaction. No average person recognized the significance of the action. All of the news

addressed the tremendous explosion and impact of the bomb on the cities and the populations. Soon, the new weapon brought the Japanese Emperor to recognize that continuing the war was futile. Over the protests of some of the Japanese military, Japan agreed to an unconditional surrender. The end of World War II ended abruptly in August, 1945.

The end of WW II was followed by the mass discharge of Americans from the military services. A point system was established that would help to determine the order of military discharges of the draftees. For example, points were awarded for the length of military service, combat actions, and various military awards. The more points a veteran was credited with, the earlier he would be discharged. My fellow soldiers and I benefited from the sudden and unexpected end of hostilities. The military training eased considerably overnight. More time was spent doing leisure type training, for example, short marches without weapons and heavy back-packs. The changes were welcomed by all of the men. The question most commonly asked by the men at the PX or at break times related to when we would be discharged. The answer to this and other questions came soon enough. All of us were advised that we would be retained in the military service for the foreseeable future, whatever that meant. We were also advised that we could possibly be sent to Japan or to Germany for occupation duty or be sent to various other posts overseas to relieve troops stationed at such places who were scheduled to be sent to the United States for discharges

and return to civilian life. The good news was that there was no combat projected for the men.

The end of the training cycle, approximately sixteen weeks, arrived quickly. The entire Regiment paraded at a nearby field to the tune of military music consisting of various marches. The Regimental Commander gave a speech that few of the men took to heart. The men were more concerned to returning to the barracks, sharing good-byes and addresses with many of their buddies with whom they became very close friends, and receiving their travel orders and furlough papers for their travel home for a deserved thirty day leave. Included in the documentation were travel orders and train tickets to their next assignment in the Army. My next assignment was Ft. Riley, Kansas.

On military leave and on the way home from Anniston, Alabama, in late September, 1945, I enjoyed the train ride, visited the dining car to enjoy my first non-army meal since May of that year, and listened to the song coming over the address system, "Sentimental Journey Home". I truly had mixed feelings. I realized that I would never again see some of the men with whom I had developed close relationships. I wondered what changes had taken place with my family in Toledo. Would some of my peacetime friends in my neighborhood be out of the military services? Then of course, I wondered what the Army had in store for me when I would report for duty at Ft. Riley. Time would weigh heavy as the train proceeded to Toledo.

Home on furlough was a joy. Life seemed to stand still. It was difficult to imagine that I had been gone for almost five months.

It was time to enjoy the peace and tranquillity of home. My mother prepared special meals for me. Polish type meals such as Polish kielbasa for lunch, czarnina soup with home made noodles (czarnina was made from the blood of a duck), potato pancakes, and other special dishes plus various Polish pastries.

I had the opportunity to meet several men who were already discharged from the military services. These were men who were drafted very early or volunteered for the military and served in combat situations. They had accumulated a high number of points awarded for their length of service and combat credits, and were back home as civilians. I was the young soldier fortunate enough to have missed the various life threatening experiences that they had encountered in Europe and in the Pacific war zones. At the time I felt somehow cheated. I had originally volunteered for immediate induction into the military with the idea, no the hope, that I would play a bigger part in the war, namely in combat. I did not fully comprehend at the time I was on leave how lucky I had been not to have seen combat. I admired the men I knew had been in combat but were now civilians that I met at Wally's Cafe, Skippy's Bar, and, yes, even on my way to St. Anthony's Church on Sunday mornings during my military leave.

The furlough time passed rapidly. It seemed as though I had never left for the Army. But, there was no doubt of my status. Each time I viewed my Army issued duffel bag and clothing, I was reminded that I was still in the Army. While home on military leave, I did learn that my mother had attended the Macomber High School commencement and received, in my

absence, my diploma. The entire family was proud. This would make it easier for me to attend college if I so desired after my Army career. Soon, too soon, I had to leave home and Toledo for my next destination, Ft. Riley, Kansas. I did not realize that my next return to Toledo would involve major differences in my life. Saying good-bye to my parents was difficult. My father was seriously ill with prostate cancer. My mother tried to stay strong. My siblings assured me that they would make certain I would be advised of my father's condition and that they would also take care of my mother. My oldest brother was recently discharged from the Navy's Seabees. He encouraged me to have a good Army tour and wished me a safe return home. Hence it was with mixed emotions that I departed for Ft. Riley, Kansas.

The train ride to Ft. Riley was uneventful. When I arrived, together with hundreds of other men, we were literally placed in a holding pattern. Apparently the Army was still going through the process of assigning the men to duty in various parts of the world. No one knew where they would be sent for further military duty. As it developed, the first men assigned to various duty stations were the married men with families. These men were given assignments to Posts, Camps, and Stations in the Continental United States (CONUS). The remainder of us were held in suspense. We had no training. It was rather boring for the men. Some of us were given light work assignments or details as we called them. I spent some time at the USO in Manhattan, Kansas, a nearby town.

Without much fanfare or warning, my name appeared on a list of men who were to report with their duffel bags for reassignment. The troop train was ready and waiting to take hundreds of us to our next destination. None of us knew where we were going. It was sort of odd. The war was over. Why the secrecy? Oh, well, we figured the Army was in a routine for years and had a difficult time breaking out of its "old ways". But, we would soon learn for ourselves at least in what direction we were traveling based on the towns we passed and, believe it or not, where the sun was setting. We were headed toward the south east. Final destination was unknown.

Two days later we arrived at Camp Picket, Virginia. This strongly suggested that we might be going to Europe. It was a boring day or two before we were again advised to report with our duffel bags ready for shipping out. The troop train headed north east, obviously to one of the sea ports. There was no question in any one's mind that we were being shipped to Europe. The big question was what country or part of Europe. The American military forces were stationed in England, France, Austria, Italy, and Germany. Perhaps even in the Netherlands. But, we did not play the guessing game. All we could do was speculate. Of course there were all sorts of rumors. This was just normal.

The transportation to the port went without any disruptions or delays. In just a matter of hours we arrived at a port in New York city. The train went directly to the loading area. We moved out of the train and proceeded to board a relatively small troop transport. It was timed perfectly. As each man moved aboard

the ship, our names were checked off a list. In just a matter of a few hours all of the troops were on the ship, assigned to bunks, and were able to go top-side to witness the ship pulling away from the dock. Our last view was of New York city, the Statue of Liberty, and the United States. I was not alone in having a little *angst* and wondered not only what the future held for me but when I would see these same beautiful sights again. I could never have guessed what the future would be for me. As the ship sailed into the distance, we lost sight of the "land of the big PX" and "the land with the round door knobs". It was the fall of 1945. We were on our way to Europe. New and interesting experiences would soon follow. None of the men on the ship could imagine the experiences they would encounter in the coming months and years. The voyage was uneventful. We were very fortunate. The sea was calm and the weather perfect throughout the entire voyage. Life would never be the same for most of the men. This was especially true for me.

A photo taken while in training at Ft. McClellan, Alabama

June, 1945

Chapter Nine
Army Life in Germany

The troop transport had smooth sailing from New York to Le Havre, France. After a few short days in a small fishing village named Etretedt, most of the men from the transport boarded a train with its destination Germany. The puzzle was solved. From a replacement depot in Germany, several of us were transported by truck to Heilbronn for a few days and than a select group of us were taken by truck to a final assignment in Ludwigsburg, Germany. This would be my home for many months. After being processed and interviewed, I was given my assignment in the 633rd Medical Clearing Company. I was placed in charge of administration of a hospital in a prisoner of war camp, Camp 78 (CI), in Zuffenhausen, Germany. I would have the weekends to travel and do things on my own. We were made aware of the American non- fraternization and wedding bans between American and German civilians. Both bans were put into effect even prior to the end WW II. The non-fraternization ban was difficult to enforce by the Army and the Military Police (MP's) due to the fact that the United States military employed hundreds of thousands of German civilians in various capacities.

The marriage ban was relatively easy to enforce. The same could not be said for the non-fraternization ban. In addition to the vast numbers of Germans employed by the Army, there were millions of displaced persons (DP's) in Germany. It was difficult for the MP's to determine if a civilian, male or female, being

accompanied by an American was in fact a German national. The fact that the American military had employed millions of Germans and DP's to work in offices, commissaries, the post exchanges, and in the military Service clubs, the contact between the Americans and civilians was constant.

My duties at the hospital were certainly not strenuous. I had a great deal of time on my hands. Preparing reports and overseeing the activities of the hospital's doctors provided time to have discussions with the hospital's staff consisting of four medical doctors, one dentist, several male nurses, and my male secretary. All of the staff were German war prisoners. All were in the German armed forces except for my secretary. He was a German civilian and was in prison for a minor war crime, that is, striking a DP worker under his supervision during the war. Our discussions involved several topics that ranged from politics, sports, life in the United States, life in Germany prior to the war as the staff remembered, and our plans after all of us returned to civilian life. All of these topics were very interesting and made for lively discussions. Interestingly, we had no language barrier. My background in the Polish-American environment in Toledo plus my ability to learn German from civilians in Ludwigsburg employed by the Company, from the Camp's hospital staff, and through association with local Germans in and around the Ludwigsburg area helped me to communicate in German. Needless to say, I could not speak fluently but my capability did allow me to understand what was being said to me. I could convey my requests and ideas when conversing with the German

barber, waiters and waitresses at the cafes, and other situations. With the exception of one of the German doctor's in the camp, all of the staff had an excellent grasp of the English language.

I spent much of my free time in Ludwigsburg playing ping-pong, visiting various sites in the city, and playing softball when the weather permitted. With the war over, it was like a holiday. I did manage to doing some skiing in the Bavarian Alps. The very first time I put on skis was at a small American recreation area name "Oberjoch". However, The big action took place during a week-end visiting Berchtesgaden, Germany, in July, 1946. With several friends, I visited Berchtesgaden. The big attractions were the mountains and "breakfast in bed". The latter was advertised by the Army Special Services to entice military personnel to visit Berchtesgaden. It was too good to believe. Together with four of my buddies we decided to spend a vacation in Berchtesgaden. On July 12 we departed Ludwigsburg for our dream week-end. We arrived in the evening, after dark. The following morning we awoke to a dream world. Looking out of our window of the Post Hotel, the hotel was operated by the Army for personnel on leave, we were taken in by the beauty of the Alps. The sun was shining, the day was bright and clear. It was truly unbelievable. In addition to the view, we were having breakfast in bed. Unheard of in the Army. I had never had breakfast served to me in bed. Not even when I was home in Toledo, sick in bed. I always had to get out of bed to have breakfast. Was this real? Our doubts vanished when the young German waitress knocked on our door and came in with our breakfast. In anticipation of this action,

my buddy and I shaved and showered knowing that we would be served in this manner. I doubt if the Army in its history had ever provided this service to its men in uniform.

After breakfast, we visited the salt mines in town. This was truly a very unique experience. We had to don black shirt, pants, and a hat. We all mounted or straddled a small rail car that took us into the mines from the street level deep into the shafts. The rail car stopped at various points in the mine including a small chapel and a small man-built lake. We crossed the lake on a small boat. It was interesting to learn of the procedure used for extracting the salt from the mine. A small shaft was dug deep into the rock. The shaft was flooded thus facilitating the absorption of the salt from the rock. The resulting "salt water" was pumped out of the mine and piped to nearby Bad Reichenhall for processing where the salt was than extracted from the water, packaged, and shipped to various parts of Germany and foreign markets. All of us were impressed with the tour. It was an unusual experience that I would never forget.

We spent the afternoon visiting the remains of Hitler's Bavarian home on Obersalzberg. The frame of the home was still standing although the entire building was gutted. All of the furniture was gone. No doubt the local natives helped themselves to the furniture and fixtures after the British bombing of the area and prior to the arrival of the Americans just a few days later. I learned several years later the structure was totally demolished primarily to keep the remnants of Hitler's home from becoming a historical site for the hard core NAZI's. Following our walk

through the home, we took a jeep to ride up to the Kehlstein to visit the guest house or tea room. The Americans retained the name of this area "The Eagle's Nest". The name still stands today even for the thousands of German and foreign tourists that visit the area each year. Tours to the Eagle's Nest are available from April until November. The specific dates are dependent on the weather conditions. There have been occasions when employees were stranded on top of the mountain due to sudden snow storms in November when the conditions were very dangerous to use the roads. Helicopters had to be used to bring the personnel into the valley. We all had a full day. Our evening was spent in the Post Hotel's dining room that was converted to a dance hall in the evenings and where we could enjoy a few beers prior to calling it a day. We had one big problem. We had no dates with any ladies, American, German, or displaced persons (DP's). But it was a day to remember. I had taken many pictures of the ruins of Hitler's home. One day I would look back at these photos and wonder if I was really there.

After breakfast (in the dining room) on Sunday, July 14, we decided to walk through the town. The Berchtesgaden restaurants and souvenir shops were open. We were again fortunate with very good weather. After lunch, we decided to visit the mountain lake, Koenigsee. One of my buddies, John C., who was driving the vehicle drove all the way to the Lake where the other fellows got out to view the beautiful scene. The Lake was surrounded by mountains. The water, crystal clear, reflected the mountains. My buddy asked me to go back with

him. I did not understand his suggestion. But, I agreed to go with him. Just a short distance from the Lake he stopped the vehicle. He pointed up on a small grassy knoll about fifty meters off the main road. There were two beautiful young ladies. We wanted female company for going dancing. We were hoping that the two young women were natives of the area so that we could learn more about Berchtesgaden. We approached the two young ladies with confidence. I was immediately attracted to one of the them. As soon as they saw that we were approaching, they rose up from the grass and started to walk away from us. There were no sidewalks. They had to walk along the side of the road. I tried to greet them in English. No answer. I tried my Polish. After all there were thousands of Polish and other foreign women in Germany as displaced persons. No answer. Admittedly, my Polish language was not very good. I tried speaking in my very limited German. Still no response. The two ladies were conversing with each other, practically whispering. I could not hear what they were saying to each other and I could not discern the language. About the time I was going to give up, an American military sedan came speeding from the direction of Koenigsee. The driver was either drunk or was driving with the intent of hitting the two girls. I pulled the two women aside and out of danger. I said to the one that attracted my interest, "At least you could say thank you". To my very pleasant surprise, she answered, "Thank you". "Aha", I replied, "Now I know that you speak English and that you understand me". At this point I knew the two girls were not displaced Polish persons and that they were German nationals.

With my best manners, I proceeded to tell her that we were in Berchtesgaden for the week-end. I further explained that this was our last night in town and all we wanted to do was to go dancing. During this conversation we were walking along the road and a long distance from our vehicle. I told the girls that we could go dancing at the Post Hotel. After introducing ourselves to the girls, I learned the name of the one who attracted me. It was Frances. Someday I would look back at this small drama and, ironically, say thanks to that idiot American driver who tried to hit the ladies and my buddy and I as we walked along the road.

Well, we did go dancing that evening at the Post Hotel. I have to admit that I never was much of a dancer. One of my sister's gave me a few lessons prior to my entry into the Army. In addition, while attending Macomber High, I was invited a few times to attend dances at Walt Whitman High sponsored by the Sports Department. I was invited due to being on Macomber's bowling team. Yes, bowling was a high school sport in Toledo. Bowling was a very popular activity throughout the Midwest in the 1930's and 1940's. However, Frances and I became deeply involved in discussing our mutual backgrounds. We talked about our hopes and ambitions. We interrupted our conversation occasionally to dance. Frances was a much better dancer than I. Of course it did not help me that I was wearing combat boots.

I learned that she was employed by the Berchtesgadener Zeitung, the town's only newspaper. She described how she obtained the position and how much she enjoyed the work. She

expressed the desire to someday travel not only within Germany and Europe but to such places as South America. I learned from our conversation that she was born and raised in the Berchtesgaden area. I was taken in by the beauty of the area in the short time I had been in the town. Fortunately, the weather was perfect and the full beauty of the area was visible. The mountains were gorgeous. I mentioned to Frances that I could not imagine anyone wanting to leave the area. It was obvious to me that this was one young lady I wanted to see again.

I spent some time explaining my background including describing not only the Toledo, Ohio, area but the United States in general. Needless to say I could describe the Western and Eastern parts of the United States only from text books, movies, or pictures due to the fact that I had never traveled to those parts myself. Those trips were in my future plans. I also mentioned that I wanted to continue my education and hoped that I could get into a career field where I could take advantage of my technical training. My target was directed toward the industrial field. This would be in an area where I believed I would find satisfaction in my work and where I could see the results of my efforts. Designing organizations, studying production techniques, analyzing methods, implementing new concepts in manufacturing processes and work simplification, installing improvements, and eventually becoming a manager in a large industrial organization were established goals of mine. Frances was very attentive during my dissertation.

The evening was outstanding. To say that I was very impressed with Frances on our first date would be a tremendous understatement. We had so much in common. We were two serious people. Our backgrounds were somewhat similar. My Polish ancestry and Frances' German background had similar characteristics and traits, for example religion, food, work habits, a desire to travel, and the need to have a good education. We both recognized that life provided many opportunities and that the future or post World War II era would bring many changes to Germany and the United states.

I mentioned to her that I would try to return to Berchtesgaden and hopefully meet with her again. She did give me her office phone number and her home address for making future contacts. After walking her home, I returned to the Post Hotel on a cloud. I knew that I would return. The non-fraternization and wedding bans would not stop me.

On Monday morning I was saddened to leave Berchtesgaden. I knew that I had found someone very special. During the return trip to Ludwigsburg I kept thinking of the previous evening with Frances. There was no question in my mind that Frances was something very special and that I would make every effort to return to Berchtesgaden and meet with Frances.

Part IV

Chapter Ten
The Long Range Courtship

I was very busy in Ludwigsburg. My work at Camp 78 kept me very active Monday through Friday. Holidays were just another work day. My mind was on Frances in Berchtesgaden. Going to our Company's club at the Stuttgarter Tor, meaning Doorway to Stuttgart, in the evenings did not have the same allure as it did prior to my visit to Berchtesgaden and meeting Frances. I was back from my visit only a few days when I decided to try to phone Frances at her office. Glory be. I was successful on the first try. This was indeed unusual due to the fact that the post WW II phone service was still archaic. I had to use a military and a civilian phone route to reach Berchtesgaden. Finally I did contact Frances. The lines were open and I was aware that the German telephone operators were eavesdropping on my call. These were not secured telephone connections. There was no doubt in my mind that I had surprised Frances with the phone call. We talked for several minutes. I mentioned that I would be visiting Berchtesgaden the coming week-end and would like to take her dancing at the Post Hotel. She was very receptive. I figured so far, so good. I talked with my buddy the 1st Sergeant and arranged to have a vehicle reserved for my trip. The days seemed to have wings. As would be the situation on all of my trips, I planned on leaving on Friday and returning to Ludwigsburg on Monday. The Company was very liberal with its leave policies. The fact that we were a small Company

and had close associations facilitated "loose" policies involving leaves. It also helped that we were proficient in our assigned military duties.

During my visits to Berchtesgaden after my first trip, I managed to stay at the Army managed and operated Bellevue Hotel. It was only a few meters away from the apartment building where Frances and her mother lived. During my second visit to Berchtesgaden, Frances suggested that we walk to the Maria Gern Church. As on my first visit to Berchtesgaden, the weather was ideal for outdoors' activity. The view of the mountains was spectacular. The walk took us through a small valley that led to a path going up a slight hill to the Church. We stopped half way to our destination to sit in the open field and had a spectacular view of the Watzmann mountain. It truly was one of the most beautiful scenes I had ever witnessed. The sky was clear of any clouds. It was as though the heavens had created a picture. No artist could have captured the view as it appeared that Saturday. As we sat in the field, we elaborated on our backgrounds and ambitions including long range goals in life. It was a special day to remember.

Frances again expressed her desires to travel to far distant places. She spoke of plans to study foreign languages. She stated that her current knowledge of the English language was helping her communicate with all of the American personnel requesting printing services from the local newspaper. Her objective was to increase her knowledge to better represent the newspaper in its business dealings with the Americans. I felt sort of stupid not

being able to converse intelligently in German. My work at the Camp did not dictate a knowledge of the German language. In fact, some of the prisoners spoke excellent English. Several of the men had spent years in the United States prior to the war on business matters. A few of the men were prisoners of war in various parts of the United States. They were captured in North Africa and shipped to the United States. There were few States that did not receive the German and Italian prisoners of war from the African campaign. Some picked cotton in Texas. Others worked in lumber operations in Washington or the Midwest. They were all well treated and enjoyed luxuries that were unavailable in their homelands during the war years. The availability of food in itself was noteworthy. Even when I tried to speak German to the men in the Camp, the prisoners would speak to me in English. They were attempting to improve "their" English. I was fighting a losing battle. My secretary, a male prisoner, spoke perfect English. He had spent several year in the United States prior to WW II as a salesman. With the exception of one of the doctors on the hospital's staff, they all spoke very good English. No doubt they had training in the English language as medical students. They also had improved their vocabularies as a result of treating the American military assigned to the Camp. For whatever reason, many of the Americans assigned to the Camp in administration, interrogators, and as guards came to the German doctors in the Camp for various treatments ranging from allergy problems to tooth aches. The doctors were not at all interested in my desire to practice my German. As a

result, the conversations between Frances and I were in English. Frances did the translating when her mother and I attempted to communicate. Later, when I would meet some of Fran's close friends, she would function as a translator. I believe she enjoyed the process. It helped her to have a stronger grasp of the English language. I have no doubt that she did tire at times from the process of translating but she never let on. It did happen more than once when she became confused and spoke to her mom in English and spoke to me in German. We had a good laugh on these occasions.

We were both saddened when Sunday evening arrived. We both knew that I would have to return to Ludwigsburg on Monday morning. Every week-end was memorable as were all of the many week-ends we would spend together in the weeks and months to come. I began to feel like a Berchtesgaden native. In time and due to the frequency of the trips to Berchtesgaden and return, I was able to memorize the train schedules.

I mentioned to Frances that I would write to her and would advise her of my next visit. The return train ride to Ludwigsburg via Munich was always heart wrenching. The sound of the train wheels passing over the tracks was like a drum beating out loud, clickety click, clickety click. Each such sound meant another few yards away from Berchtesaden and Frances. And with it, my heart would hurt. The sound would have a reverse impact when I was on my way back to Berchtesgaden for a visit. I knew that my feelings for Frances ran deep and that I was "captured" by her character, yes, looks, and certainly our mutual interests.

We were obviously two serious people. I began writing letters to Frances between my visits. I gave her my civilian address in Ludwigsburg so that she could write to me using the German postal system. The letters were not masterful in respect to the English and spelling. At the time, they were however truly descriptive of our mutual feelings. As we would often review these letters in the future, we do have two books of the letters that were bound by a German book-binder employed by the newspaper, our hearts would light up. It is hard to imagine that our words were put on paper more than five decades ago. However long, it worked out fine. I have no doubt if with the passing years Frances and I, for whatever reason, would need to correspond the thoughts and ideas expressed in both of our letters would be the same today with improved spelling and vocabularies. Of course, many of our letters were hand written while still others were typed on pre-WW II typewriters. Frankly, correct spelling and grammar were the last items on our minds. Communication took precedence.

Between my visits to Berchtesgaden, I was also busy in sports. Playing tennis was a good outlet. The Company arranged to have intramural softball games that entertained all of the troops. Even the officers participated. It was like a commercial company or business back in the States where the employees would gather to play softball on a week-end. It was one big happy family. Everyone appreciated the exercise and comradeship after the game.

During my visits with Frances, we always tried to go dancing on Saturday evenings and occasionally on Sunday evenings. We spent the Saturdays and Sundays taking walks in the area. An outstanding feature of Berchtesgaden are the many trails and sites that can be visited while in the area. If the weather cooperates, i.e., sunshine and clear skies, there are outstanding walks accessible to anyone who wants to take in the scenery, enjoy the outdoors, and not have to worry about wild animals or poisonous snakes. The Bavarian environment could not be any healthier.

I especially enjoyed the walks to Koenigsee. The path to Koenigsee follows the river flowing from the lake. It is a scenic view from beginning to end. The approach to the Lake is something special. In late 1945, the Americans had erected a sign just outside of the Lake area that read, "Slow, Men Resting". The sign has disappeared many years ago but the idea still applies to the Lake area. It is a peaceful setting and certainly a place to rest mind, body, and soul.

On one of my subsequent visits, Frances took me for a long walk to the Almbach Klamm, it was a gorge with a fast mountain stream cascading from the very top to the bottom. We were able to walk from the town to the Klamm and then proceeded to walk up one side of the gorge to the top. This was a beautiful view. I especially enjoyed watching the trout feeding at the bottom of the many pools that dotted the gorge. This was nothing like the Maumee River flowing through Toledo or Lake Erie. I never envisioned being able to fish for trout. The fishing in the Toledo

area was great for perch, walleyes, catfish, and several other varieties of fish. But not fresh water trout. If there were such places in the area, I was not aware of them.

We were again fortunate to have outstanding weather. Of course, it goes without saying that in order to enjoy any outdoor activities, the weather has to cooperate. In order to have an appreciation of the beauty of any mountain area, be it the Rockies or Alps, it helps to have a clear day, without too much cloud cover. The entire walk took us the better part of five hours. It was a typical day for Frances and I whenever I had the opportunity to visit her in Berchtesgaden. I was extremely fortunate to be assigned to a military unit that was small enough for everyone to know each other and to have a close relationship. Thanks to the understanding of Jim, the 1st Sergeant, I was able to have a free hand in visiting Berchtesgaden. Jim knew that I was serious about Frances. He went out of his way to allow me to make frequent trips to visit with Fran. He was an outstanding friend.

During the days that I was unable to visit Berchtesgaden and there were many, too many as far as I was concerned, Frances and I communicated by mail. There were occasions when I would find myself writing two, even three letters a day.

In September, I was informed that I would no longer be reporting for duty at Camp 78. The administration of all of the prisoner of war facilities in the Ludwigsburg area were being turned over to the German Government. Camp 78 was one of these facilities. I was assigned to two new duties. I became the

acting mess sergeant. Great duty for a man who never in his life was capable of frying an egg or making a pot of coffee. My mother or one of my sisters took care of all of my dining needs. But, the 633rd Medical Clearing Company had this vacancy and I happened to be available. I was told that I needn't worry. There was a German local national (LN) as the chief cook and he was ably assisted by a Hungarian national who was a displaced person. The entire staff of the mess hall was comprised of German and Polish and Hungarian displaced persons, all civilians. I was the only American assigned to the mess hall. My principal duty was to pick up the weekly food rations from a central point in Ludwigsburg. I also had the responsibility for making certain that the food rations were not pilfered. I had no problems with either of these duties. There was no doubt in anyone's mind that I was in no position to prepare menus, cook, or perform the duties of a qualified mess sergeant, so the German chef took care of all of these functions.

I was also given another assignment as director of sports for the Company. I certainly enjoyed this challenge. The majority of the men in the organization were young and athletic. I had no problem arranging various sports activities for the unit. Even with this added activity, I still had time to spare. I took advantage of this free time to write letters home to my family in Toledo and to Frances. It gave me time to think about my future and my love for Frances. I resolved to ask her to marry me. Of course, there were the non-fraternization and wedding bans. I became convinced that I would propose marriage to Frances the

next time we met. If she would acquiesce, I believed she would, I would then concentrate on overcoming both bans. I knew that the wedding ban would pose the major problem. Thus began an unusual series of events and actions that would have profound impacts on the lives of Frances and I. In one of my letters, I addressed the fact that I had an important question to present to her at our next meeting in Berchtesgaden.

Near the end of August and the beginning of September, 1946, the Stars and Stripes, the unofficial Army newspaper, announced that all drafted personnel would be out of the European Theater of Operations by January 1, 1947. This was shocking news to me and many other American personnel who wanted to marry German girls. The Army would replace all of the draftees with enlisted personnel. I knew that this new policy would definitely have an impact on me. During my next visit to Berchtesgaden, Frances and I went walking to Maria Gern. We stopped in a field to view the mountains, as we so often did on the previous visits. As we sat in the field taking in the view, I reminded Frances that as I had stated in my last letter, I had an important question to ask. I asked her to marry me. I reminded her of the existing Army wedding ban forbidding American personnel to marry German nationals and told her that the future could pose serious problems for us in consideration of the recent published Army policy involving draftees. To my delight, Frances said "yes". She went on to say that we would face the future and any problems together. First things first, we were in love and on our voyage to a life together. Upon returning to her apartment, I asked her

mother for permission to marry her daughter. She asked me to promise to always take care of Frances. I had no problem with assuring her that I would always love, honor, and respect Fran. We spent the Sunday of our special week-end taking a long walk to the beautiful and very scenic Koenigsee. I returned to Ludwigsburg the following morning full of hope that everything would work out well. Upon returning to Ludwigsburg, the 1st Sergeant contacted me and gave me sobering news. The Company had to start preparing a list of its draftees for preparation for shipment to the United States and subsequent discharge from the Army. The shipments would be in several increments in order not to jeopardize the Company's operations. Jim agreed to save me for the last increment. We were buying time. I informed Jim of my engagement to marry. He offered his congratulations and wished us luck. Jim and I discussed several alternatives if the Army would not cancel its marriage ban and if I were be faced with having to be sent home without Frances. The first option would be to try to obtain civilian employment with the Army of Occupation in Germany. The Army was hiring American civilians in various capacities to work in supply, procurement, the Army's Post Exchange (PX) system, and other categories. There was also the option of enlisting in the Army for one year, three years, or five years. Obtaining employment with the Army was obviously the best option available to me. This would be my target. In the interim, I was able to visit Frances at least every second week-end. Our correspondence kept the German post office personnel busy.

I did have some leads on a couple of civilian job opportunities in Stuttgart, Germany, with the PX system. However, the interviews did not evolve into a position with the system. I was advised that it possibly could develop after January 1, 1947. I could not accommodate this schedule. It appeared that my solution would have to be enlisting in the Army for the shortest period, i.e., one year. I would be buying time, hoping that the military would change its policies and that Fran and I would be able to marry.

My visits to Berchtesgaden were always outstanding. Having been accepted by Fran's mother, relatives, and friends was heart warming. It was ironic in a way. Many Germans objected to German/American relationships. It was the same with some of the Americans. Some of the men in my Company were not bashful in telling me that I should not be marrying a German. It was very obvious that both the German and American involved in a romantic relationship would be criticized. I did know a few Polish girls (DP's) who tried to get me to drop the idea of marrying a German girl. In fact, one of the Polish girls went out of her way to take me to her dormitory to introduce me to several Polish girls whom she thought would make good wives.

I learned at one of my visits to Bechtesgaden that the office personnel where Frances was to apply for a passport and visa to visit the United States would not even talk to her. This was an option if I would be forced to return to the United States and would then try to bring her to Toledo. I knew that if we decided I would return to the United States without Frances and

then send for her, she would not be supported by the authorities responsible for issuing visas. Upon hearing this I stormed into the American Military Governor's Office. It was one big mistake. I should have been more considerate.

Every town had an Army Officer assigned to the position of the Military Governor (MG). The MG was the judge and jury in the town. After WW II there was no civilian authority in Germany. The Americans established the position of MG to function in its place. For the most part, it was effective. I determined that if I could talk to the MG, in this instance it was a Major, I might obtain some cooperation from the local authorities to issue Frances a visa. Well, it became obvious very quickly to me that the Major did not appreciate a mere sergeant coming into his office and demanding something be done. The Major was shocked at my audacity and in no uncertain terms told me leave his office and never return. This convinced me that my only option was to stay in Germany until I could take Frances with me to the United States. The die was cast.

Upon returning to Ludwigsburg, I was advised that it would be necessary for me to extend my tour in Germany for ninety days. This would assure my continued assignment in Germany until January 1, 1947. However, if I did not receive a Department of Army civilian status, i.e., an employee of the United States Army, or if I did not enlist in the Regular Army (RA), I would have to be on my way out of the European Theater prior to January 1, 1947. The noose was tightening. I realized that I was very fortunate to be assigned to a small Army unit and to have a

close relationship with the 1st Sergeant and the sympathy of the Commanding Officer. As winter approached and decision time came on a course of action, I decided that it was best to exercise the one remaining option and that was to enlist in the Army for one year. I knew that I could not leave Germany without 100 per cent assurance that Frances and I would be together.

During my next visit to Berchtesgaden at the beginning of December, 1946, I told Frances of my plans. We enjoyed our week-end feeling satisfied that we would definitely be together for Christmas. The weather was too cold for taking long walks in the mountains or even to Koenigsee. We took short walks to Maria Gern and along paths that surrounded the town. Saturday evening we went dancing at the Post Hotel. As usual we were welcomed by our friend the American civilian manager, who was formerly a 1st Sergeant. We became very good friends. Not only did we become somewhat of permanent fixtures at the hotel when I was visiting Frances but he also met Frances during the week when he visited the newspaper office to have his menus and other schedules printed. Similar to all of our week-ends, Sunday nights were spent at her apartment with her mom discussing future plans. I mentioned to Frances that I would come to Berchtesgaden for the Christmas and New Year Holidays. Of course, I was presumptuous. I always assumed that the Company would continue to give me tremendous freedom in my visits to Berchtesgaden. Monday morning came too fast. I would have to leave for Ludwigsburg. I knew that I had a lot to

do to make certain that I would spend the coming Holidays with Frances and her mom.

Upon my return to Ludwigsburg in early December, I immediately went to see Jim, the 1st Sergeant. We discussed the various options open to me. We also spent some time addressing the wedding ban and its impact on the all of the American military men who wanted to marry German nationals. Jim stated that he heard rumors of a possible easing of the ban and perhaps even a total rescission of the ban. But these were only rumors. I decided that it was best for me to enlist in the Army for one year. This would provide some time for men like myself to decide on various courses of action. The goal was to address the immediate problem. With this item settled, Jim would make arrangements for me to enlist in the Army. Concurrently, he indicated that I would have no problem obtaining a two week leave to visit Berchtesgaden over the coming Christmas and New Year Holidays. I tried to contact Frances to advise her of my decisions and plans but the phone lines were inoperative. This happened frequently due to the destruction of the power lines during WW II and the subsequent problems of maintenance. I wrote a brief letter hoping that she would receive it prior to my arrival in town. On December 19, 1946, I received my Honorable Discharge as a draftee from the United States Army. On the very same day, I was recorded as enlisted on December 20, 1946, in the United States Army for one year. This all happened in Esslingen, Germany. With this action completed, I was ready for my two weeks vacation in Berchtesgaden, Germany. This

visit would not only be one full of pleasant memories but would also result in a dramatic piece of good fortune that would be impossible to foresee. I gathered my personal items and thanked Jim for his assistance. I departed for Berchtesgaden full of hope and confidence. I could not believe the recent turn of events in my life. I was full of hope that the wedding ban would soon be lifted permitting Frances and I to be married and for the beginning of our new lives in the United States. Many questions still remained, e.g., would we settle in Toledo and what career path would I choose after leaving the Army. But the immediate problem was waiting for the wedding ban to be lifted. The other questions and problems would be addressed in due time. We had no doubt that there would be many challenges presented together with the lifting of the ban.

I wrote home to my family in Toledo advising them of my actions and asked for their blessings and understanding. I knew that my mother and siblings were anxious for my return to Toledo. My father had passed away while I was in Germany. There were anxieties on both sides of the Atlantic Ocean. Of course, Frances had apprehensions. Primarily they were related to acceptance by my family and friends. I tried to ease her feelings by mentioning that the United States had a large percentage of Germans who had migrated from Germany to the United States in the 19th and early part of the 20th Century. I knew Toledo had thousands of citizens of German origin. This seemed to make Frances more comfortable. Of course, one issue we discussed frequently was the impact of her leaving Germany,

her mother, and close friends. This would be the real challenge for Frances.

Following are several copies of letters between Fran and I. These letters are indicative, exemplary it could be stated, of the dozens of letters that were transmitted between us after we met in Berchtesgaden and while I was stationed in Ludwigsburg. The letters were all forwarded via the German postal system.

Aug. 2, 1946
Ludwigsburg, Germany

A letter to the sweetest girl in the world.

Dear Francis,

I hope this letter finds you feeling well, honey. I'm getting along swell, except that I miss you.

I tried telephoning you this morning. I reached Berchtesgaden, but I didn't have your number. Please send the number to me so that I may be able to phone you in the future. You can expect a call from me always in the morning, about ten o'clock.

I'm verry sure I may get a pass to visit you again within two weeks from to-day. I can hardly wait to see, the most beautiful girl in Berchtesgaden, you.

I hope you have sent me your picture. I'm going to take as many pictures of you as I possibly can the next time I see you.

Please say hello to Hilda for me.

I hope you are not working too hard. Save all your energy until I come to visit you. The next time I come I'm going to try to be with you every minute. I'll even go to work with you, if your boss doesn't object, ha, ha.

Every time I think of you I always seem to see you in that verry beautiful green dress that you wore the first night you and I were together. You were the prettiest dressed girl in Berchtesgaden that night.

I wish I could see you every night. Maybe I will if everything works out right.

Well, until the next time sweet, please answer soon.

With all my love,

Melvin

P.S.
Please excuse any errors you may find in this letter, I'm thinking too much of you.

Berchtesgaden,
5 th August 1946

Dear Melvin,

J thank you so very much for your lines J received yesterday. J have been so very happy in reading your truly words and still J feel lucky of your gentleness you showed to me. You are a very fine man and J enjoyed so much having been in your company. One week ago we were spending a nice evening in dancing and you surprised me so much in telling me about your Love and longing for our mountains and our country. Then J was very pleased to hear, that you found in that german doctor a person, who with whom you can talk of us and of whom you were learning our mode of living, our oppinions, and love. Then J felt in my heart an aquainted connection to you and still J feel glad about it.

Hilda and me are going to Ludwigsburg on Monday 19 th inst. and we are already dreaming of that coming time. Hilda was very pleased to learn, that she will get a letter from Johnny soon. Please can you get a double bedroom for us ? J learnd my aquaintance there moved to Stuttgart, so that the distance would be too far. Today already I like to thinking , that we will have a very nice time, then J will be enjoying your progresses in dancing. Besides that J am very curious to learn that important something you will be talking about to me.

My dear, J am expecting your next very soon. May-be we will have that luck to see us befor in Berchtesgaden.

Meanwhile J remain with love

Yours Francis

Sorry, now J have not any picture of me, perhapes we can take one in Ludwigsburg.

Berchtesgaden, 2 Sept 46

My dearest Melv,

J guess your ears must burn for J am thinking so very very much of you. J cannot explain how sad J was when we parted at the train yesterday. What a pity that we were in such hurry. The whole trip J felt so sorry and rather J wanted to jump out and go back to you. When J left Berchtesgaden J didn't think J ever would love you so much than J am doing now. J fe am feeling like sick today and could cry like a child. Although J found here much work to do J can be sitting doing nothing only thinking of you and the wonderful time we spent together. J remember every detail of our talking, loving, walking, everything, o Melv. What will you be doing and thinking and how did you feel yesterday ? Although J have my home here and J have a very dear mother, J feel like a stranger here, because J miss you at any time and place.

Now J realize more and more, that we have to pray and beg God for so many things. J am thinking of tomottow, when you will be going to Heidelberg and work out the things rightly. J almost cannot wait until J get your message about this importend matter and if it will be right J don't know yet how to thank.

Mama thanks you so very much for the very fine handkerchiefs and for your greetings in our letter and J shall tell you, she will be very pleased to see you in our home.

And J want to thank you so very much for everything you have done and given to me and Hilde and J beg you to excuse my beeing late in telling. As we were so hastening yesterday J have forgotten that. J cannot thank enough in words J will send you thousend of my sweetest kisses to you.

Please tell Johnny Cr. much hallo from Hilda and our best wishes for his voyage and going home. Today morning J gave Johnnys (Kraut) letter to Rosie she was very glad to receive his writing. Please tell hallo to " Spitzfrau Pitz" and Mama of the Club.

Mamas and Hildas regards to you.

My darling J relay on you in everything and hope J can hold you tight very soon. My love for you and God shall bless you and let you stay with me.

Yours

Francis

Franzl Ponn

3.9.46

Dearest,

Just a few lines for you darling as I feel I want a little bit talk with you. I miss you and every minute we talked together so very much and am thinking all day of you. It is late in the evening and until now I had much work to do, so I am still busy and please you wouldn't be afraid that I should do anything wrong. I am so happy in thinking you belong to me and can hardly wait to see you again and for always. Today it is Wednesday I was supposed to get a telegram or a phone-call. I am sorry I got neither and I am afraid, that you couldn't reach anything at Heidelberg. If it would be going wrong I don't know yet, what I should do then.

The autumn here is vonderful. I vish you vould be here and ve could ~~the~~ see that beauty together. Dont you to go vith me in the mountains once and pray vith me there? O Melv, I vish so very much you vould be here ~~almost~~ already. I am afraid of the future, people are speaking always of var, var and var.

I am not coward but scared something could happen and part us.

May be tomorrow when I vill get your letter, I hope I vill I feel better.

There I have a little coloured picture of Bertle garden in the front to the right you see that house where I am living. Behind them you see the second building of the Hotel Bellevue. You can put it on your table and visit me a

Darling I hope you are vell and you can vork out everything rightly. In love

Yours

Francis

Excuse my vriting, it is 10 o'clock in the evening

Sept. 15,1946
Ludwigsburg,Germany

My Darling Francis,

I can't help telling you how pretty you are,in my letters. I always see your beautyful face before me. I have all the pictures of you setting on my desk before me when I write to you.

Darling,remember when I told you of one of my sisters,the one that is a widow? I wrote to her about you and I. I received an answer to-day. She said many things,all good. One thing she stressed in her letter was that you are "Catholic". Another point was what I told you once before......That it is true love on both sides. Francis, I find it verry hard to tell you how verry much I love you.I have said,and written,how much I love you many times. I was serious every time. If you love me as much as I love you,darling,nothing in the world will ever part us.

She said she can hardly wait to see you. When she does meet you and sees how wonderful you are,I'm sure she will love you as much as I do. She also has asked me to say "hello" to you for her. We have gained another praying partner,darling. She will be praying for us.

She has asked me for your ADRESS,Francis. She wants to write to you. I thought I had better ask you before I send it,is it all right with you,darling?

Please,tell me what you think,honey.

Give my love to Mom. Please,Francis, if you haven't told her all about you and I,tell her now. Tell her that I love you and that we are engaged to be married. I love you ,Francis.

Until to-morrow,darling. May God be with you.

Forever yours,

Melvin

16 Sept 46

Bonn

O darling mio,

I am ashamed in many cases. I was worrying again that the Army could get you to leave, and I was depressed until this noon when I received three of your wonderfull letters, special the one of Friday. There you wrote of signing for 6 months. Now I am really happy, so I haven't to doubt, whether I will see you once again for the leave at Stuttgart was so terrible and then I got a felling like I would see you no more. But now I am so happy. I never double on you but I thought in some ways you could be powerless. I wish we will see us soon, may-be this week-end darling. And I wish so much that you and mom will be getting to know another well. – Last Saturday I got your letter from Tuesday and I was again depressed in your telling me that you returned disappointed from Heidelberg in no getting a job at the present time. On the other hand I got your phone call Wednesday that everything got o.K. – After getting your Tuesday letter but I got sad and supposed I under stood you wrong at the phone. I could hardly

renzi Ponn

vait for your vriting. Now I got it black on vhite
that you signed. But darling, do I understand
rightly, you signed for the time, didn't you?
And during the following months the affairs about
your job will be automaticaly regulated. Please
tell me particulares. – I have to thank, thank and
again to thank you for everything.
And number two: We received your vonderfull
box this morning, like a christmas-gift. We
didn't know shall we be laughing oder crying
of thankfullness. I cannot put my and Mamas
thank in to words. We looked at the vonderful things
like two children underneath the christmas tree
and I was so very very happy when I saw Mama's
shining eyes of joy and thank. But Melo,
I didn't ask for so many things and I
and Mama are ashamed in accepting them.
Mama is afraid, you will lack the things and
may-be you will be hungry. – You cannot
imagine what you did and if you will be here,
Mama will thank you so much personally.

[illegible] please be never disappointed, if once
[illegible] you willn't get a letter. But some-
[illegible] I cannot help. In my spare-time I
[illegible] to do so many things, washing, iron, mend,
[illegible], go to dressmaker, hairmaker, dentist,
shopping. Saturday I came back from shopping
[illegible] for wintertime 11 o'clock in night.
Sunday forenoon I was again getting a little
walk. Afternoon I was at the movie "Remember
the day". I am still impressed. Did you
see it. You should. It reminds me so much
of our furlough. Afterwards I had to think
so much. Then I visited Rosie for a little time.

I love you, Ich liebe Dich!
Until tomorrow darling my sweetest kiss
and my love. Mamas and Hildas heartiliest
greetings.
I thank you for the both pictures, What is wrong
with them? What is matter with the film?

Only Yours

Francis

The evening of Sept.16,1946
Ludwigsburg,Germany

To my future <u>wife</u>.

Dearest Darling Francis,

I'm the happiest man in world to-night,darling. We are getting more men to-morrow. <u>That means I will be able to come to Berchtesgaden this week-end.</u>

Oh,Francis, I can hardly wait until Friday when I leave. I'm going to kiss and hug you until my arms ache. I have prayed verry hard that I would be able to see you verry soon. My prayers have been answerd.

I want you to know that I shave often. I want to look nice even when I see you in my dreams,which has been verry often also. Daling,when I come to see you I'm going to shave every day. I don't ever want to hurt you.

I miss you verry much ,dearest. I'm going to be like a child until I see you. I love you, I love you, I love you, I love you, I love you, I love you.

Gee,honey,if I could only explain to you on paper what you mean to me. Just wait until I see you , I'm going to kiss you like you have never been kissed before. I feel rough to - night,darling. I feel like I could fly to you.

Just think,Francis,five nights from to - day I will be with you. My God,darling,it is like a beautiful dream. With you being the "Star".

Please,say "hello" to Mom for me. I can hardly wait to see her too. I have an important question to ask her.

Until to - morrow,sweetheart,may God watch over you and Mother for me. Sweet dreams , Darling.

With all the love in the world,

Melvin

P.S.
I'm learning German like "mad",Honey.

Sept. 25,1946
Ludwigsburg,Germany

earest Darling of Mine,

Just two more days,Honey, and then you and I will be to-gether once again. ee! you are so verry nice,Francis. I love you so verrry much.

Daling, I can hardly wait until we will be living in America. You and I, e, will always be happy. You will be the fairest lady in the land. You will be my ife. I shall always love you.

Darling,last night I searched the sky for our group of stars. They seemed o be the only planets in sight. I thought of you,Honey,and of the wonderful things ou and I have done to-gether. I thought of walks we took to-gether,of the times we anced with one another, and a million other things that contributed to our love.

I am learning to say "I love You" in French now,Darling.. That is one more anguage in which I can say I LOVE YOU.

When I see you Friday I am going to kiss you like you have never been kiss- d before,Honey. Be careful of me, I am going to be rough .

Please,say "hello" to Mother for me. Tell her I am looking forward to see- ing her Friday.

I am praying we will have fine weather so that you and I can go walking to-gether,Darling. We will go to the same place where we went the last time. I want to be able to look at the beautiful mountains and to talk with you,to tell you how much I love you. Oh! Darling, you will be mine always.

Until to-morrow ,Francis,sleep well and may God watch over you.

Only yours,

Melvin

P.S.

I love You.

Oct. 3,1946
Ludwigsburg,Germany

y Dearest Darling Franzi,

I am sorry I was unable to telephone you yesterday,Honey,I could not ake the connection. I didn't have a chance to tell you I willbe with you this eek-end. I can hardly wait to see you again , Franzi.

John will accompany me. By the time you receive this letter, Honey , e will have spent either all ,or part, of our week-end to-gether.

I received your wonderful letter from the first of this month. I am t a loss to express my feelings when I receive your mail,Honey. Boy! I could ump as high as the sky when Frau Pitz tells me I have a letter from you.

Someday,Honey,we will never have towrry about when we will see one another again. We will be to-gether always. I pray that the day is not far off.

I feel mean when I thought of how I insisted that you write to me very day,Honey,please don't be angry at me for asking you to do it..I want o hear your voice and your letters help me so very much. I pretend that you re saying to me what is written in your notes.

I love you, I love you, I love you, I love you, Ilove you.........

Please give my love to Mom. I hope she won't get disgusted of eeing me around so often..I don't want to make her angry at me,Honey..

At the time you receive this letter ,Sweet, I will be with you. ntil the next time,Franzi,May God be with you always.

I'll love you forever and
remain yours always,

Melvin

Oct. 9,1946
Ludwigsburg,Germany

Dearest Darling Franzi,

I am elready lobking forward to our next meeting,Honey. I am almost positive that I will be able to visit you again this weekend,Franzi.

Yesterday,on our way back from Berchtesgaden,I was the only one out of the fellows who was warm. I thought of you all the way back. Every time I leave you ,Honey the action of yours always make an impression on my mind. This time it was when you stomped your foot on the floor and cried. Honey, I love you more every time I see you.

Please,say hello to Mom for me. Give her my love.

I hope we will have good weather the next time I visit you, Honey. I want to visit the church onthe hillside with you,again. I want to do so many things I don't know where to begin . The most important of them all is to marry you. I love you.

Honey, I want to thank you for getting into my dreams. There is only one thing about it, Sweet, that is my disappointment when I awake.

I am going to Heidelberg either to-morrow or Thursday. I will be praying that everything will go along well.

I received your letter from last week Thursday, Honey. I don't know how to express my feelings when I receive one of your letters,Franzi. I look forward to receiving them everyday.

We probably will take an ambulance to Berchtesgaden this weekend. It will make the trip more pleasant for those accompaning Johnny and myself. We, John and I, don't care what we go in, we would evenwalk.

Until to-morrow's letter ,Honey, Sweet dreams and may God help us.

Your swindler,
and Gangster,

Melvin
(Bunny)

Franzi Ponn | Berchtesgaden, den 6.XI.46.

My dearest Bommy,

A few hours ago we were happy in talking to one another at the phone. And I am looking forward already, talking we to you tomorrow again.
My dearest Melvin, can it be true, you will become a civilian almost positive within a few weeks. — ?
I want to thank God for what He did for us still now and ask Him for His help in future.

It is Wednesday evening again. If you should be able to be down here this week-end, so I [illegible] got only 2 days more to count, otherwise 10 days yet, until we will meet us. I am very happy.
Since you left it has been raining. It seems, that only those Sundays you will be here as my dearest guest, the sun will be shining.
How is my sleepy boy? Are you still going to bed at 8 o'clock?
We thank you heartiliest for the very, very fine and useful things we received today. And we want to thank God too. Mom told me she paid a mass and is also thanking and praying for us in addition.
Very soon I will be going to bed, I should like to get a wonderful dream. Good night, darling, until tomorrow. I am thinking of you.

Yours,
Honey.

Excuse the awful writing.

…anzi Ponn

Berchtesgaden
10.XI.46.

To my darling:

Sunday evening. My dear, I hope it didn't any thing bad happen, I am scared as I didn't get your phonecall Saturday for which I was waiting very hard. But may be you couldn't get the connection. Perhapes I know more about tomorrow noon. – Last night I was listening to music of operettes and songs of love by our radio. Listening to them my heart is getting very softly. If I wouldn't be ashamed, I sometimes could start crying, thinking of beeing happy loving a person like you and longing. Then each picture is passing of our very good time we spent together.
Today 1.30 I heard true bavarian music, may-be you were listening at the same time too. I thought of you, how much you like that music. In the afternoon I attended with Mam, Hilda and Anni "The Sullivans", an wonderful movie. We are still impressed. Did you see it once, darling? The five little boys were the delight of everybody. And the happy marriage of their Mam and Dad and the hard times they had with their alive kids. Looking at the youngest one, whom I loved best,

I pictured you my darling, when you were a boy about five years old. & Bonny-boy I love you very much.

I miss you very much. A Sunday again. That day it reminds me most of you, that day, we always could spent the most time together. Each thing in our room reminds me of you. And what will darling be doing? And how will you feel? How is your Mom and your family? Have you any cares my dear? Please let me ever know.

And what about my enthusiastic democrate? My darling, I guess, you got a problem for your future. To convince your peopel and them of your oppositionsparty too of the good ideas of the democrates, that once that will be elected for the first again. I know, you always would representative good, human ideas.

Mom is again already sitting at the stove. Also she misses you so much. And she hasn't any chance to improve her English! And nobody is grooling! Boy, but I am cold, but my heart is very warm. It hoo possesses the best fire.

My darling, I am waiting for you. Please come soon very soon. I am thinking of you. I kiss my Bonny good night.

Yours
Franci..

From Mam I shall tell you: "Hilde* ist in Ordnung?", because you were just like his red-head.

ranzl Ponn

Berchtesgaden
13.11.46.

Mein geliebter Melvin!

Your letters, each one, made me very happy. I cannot thank enough. They are meaning so very much to me. Reading your very dear words I just mean you express my own feeling and thinking in it. You wrote to me that way I would do it to you. Only my language isn't not that perfect.

Also I got the clipping of your fathers death. My dear, I can imagine how sad you must be feeling specially when you are alone. How is your Mom? I will learn it this week end, I hope. – In addition I received the pictures today. They aren't too bad, but dearest, what did you do, you cut my head twice. Where did you put the other half of my head?

My darling, I was very happy getting your phone call yesterday. O God, I may hope to see you this weekend. I pray I will'nt be disappointed. Please, be a big swindler, I honest don't blame you. – Today the phone was awful quiet.

I suppose you didn't come through.

My darling, please excuse making short this writing. I have been very busy for a few days. I had to move out of my little office. It will become a dwelling-room for our boss. So I had to move into his office opposite the Post Hotel. He is around me at any time. At home is waiting a big basket of washings to be mend. I do everything with pleasure, thinking I will see you soon again

O darling mio. I am praying hard every thing will be allright in future.

Tomorrow my dear I hope to get your ring and I should like hear you saying „I am with you this Friday.

Mam wants to hug her son too. She and I have been talking of you every day.

Much hello from Anni & Hilda.

Please say hello to Pet and Frau Pietz. She made much noise when you were phoning me last Friday. But I am not angry with her. Also she reminds me of the time with you at Ludwigsburg.

Only Yours

Franci

November 21,1946
Ludwigeburg,Germany

st Darling Franzi,

Oh !Franzi,remember several weeks ago when I visited you,you said you wanted to e with a "stomach ache" so that you dould caress and comfort me ? Well,Honey, this ng I awoke with the most terrible ache in my stomach. I ate something that didn't with me. After I was in pain a while,I couldn't help but smile to myself. I tho- of how you would love being with me at that moment.

At present I am feeling fine ,Franzi.

I spoke to o ur special service sergeant,about a pass and a furlough. I will le to get a pass to visit you on your birthday,Honey. John and I will be able to Berchtesgaden Christmas also. Now all we have to do is pray that we get our jobs. for that every evening,Honey,before going to bed. I even pray through the day t comes to my mind.

I hope you and Mom are feeling well,Darling. How is everything,Honey ? Does Mr. bother you ? Please,tell me if he does.

Across the steet from our kitchen,the Germans have a school for orphans. Every- ee them, they number about 16 or 20. The're very young. I believe they average in from 2 to 5 years. I talked to some of the fellows about having a Christmas party m. We will invite them over for Cristmas Day. I told Carl already to have cookies, and a few other things made.

I won't be here,I'll be in Berchtesgaden with you on Christmas. I love you,Honey. o be with you and Mom,because in all probability it will be your last Christmas ny(unless we visit after we are married).

Please, give my love to Mom. Tell her I will miss being with you two this week-end. iss your wonderful meals. I shall be thinking of our last week-end,Honey. I will ering you. I want to be an Apron String Boy, your apron string boy.

ntil to-night ,Sweethearth, May God Bless and Protect you evry moment of your life. Please,inform me of your visit to the docter.

Your loving Bummy boy,

Melvin

Kocham bardzo wiele.

December 11,1946
Ludwigsburg,Germany

est Darling Franzi,

I just finished talking with the sweetest girl in the world. She lives in Ber-
sgaden also,she even has a similar name. She is the most wonderful fiancee in the
d. I love you very much,Franzi. I will be looking foreward to receiving your letter
you had sent to me yesterday. I know it will be filled with words that mean so
to you and I.

Thank you for getting into my dreams. I think of you always,Honey. There isn't
ngle moment that goes past without you entering my mind. I want to think of you as
as I possibly can. It makes me feel as though I own the world. Maybe it is be-
e I know you are mine.

I went to Esligton to-day to get the necessary information on my furlough.

I am waiting impatiently for the day that I may leave on my long visit to you.
ll do so many things to-gether ,we'll become very welllacquanted with each other.

I hope this letter will find you and Mom in the best of health. I amfeeling
Please,give my love to Mom, I will miss her very much while we are parted. She
become a part of me. I feel as though she is truly my mother. I wish there could
way that we ,you,I,and Mom,could be to-gether for always. I know she is giving
great deal,when I think of the many years she has spent with you,I can understand
eelings when she first heard the words that I wanted you for my wife. I will never
le to express my thanks to her,for being so understanding and kind.

I will always keep Mom in mind,as the person who brought you into the world and
ave you to me.

I hope we will have much snow wheh I come to Berchtesgaden for my furlough.
ll have a wonderful time.

Until to-night,my Darling, May god Bless and Protect you always.

Your Darling,

Melvin

e you very much, Honey.

Dec. 12, 1946
Ludwigsburg, Germany

...e Darling Franzi,

This letter contains two things, Honey, that I am anxious to let you know.
John and I will get our furlough for Christmas and New Year. The fur-
will begin Dec. 23 (we will leave for Berchtesgaden on the 21, in the morn-
...ll be able to stay until the 5th of Jan. (we will have to leave on that day).
...ll give us 14 days with each other, and 15 evenings. Boy! we'll have
...ful time.
The other thing, and most important for you and I, is that they will
...e marriage ban on the 1st of Jan. The news came over the radio yester-
I didn't hear the news, myself, but several fellows who are engaged to
...er here, heard it. One of them, is Austin. So, I know they were telling
...uth. I will probably hear the news later in the day, and also read of
...e paper.

Oh! Honey, the day may be even sooner than you and I had expected,
...ferring to our wedding day. We will probably be allowed to marry here, in
We'll get married in Berchtesgaden!

I'll inform you briefly over the telephone to-day, of these two things.
...hardly sit still, in one place, ever since I found out that that, and
...portant factor.

t looks as if everything is going to be better than you and I have ever
o it could be. I have been praying to God so that all would be well.
me to be answering our prayers, Honey.
Please, give my love to Mom. Also, tell her of the news, Franzi.
John and I will still try to get our jobs. We want to have things settled.
e everything will be alright in the end. It has to be, my Darling. I love
ery much. All I ask is to be with you for always. You will be, Honey,
Blick.
John and I are as happy as two children. We have good reason to be,
thing is going along very well.
I hope you are well, Franzi. Is everything fine with you? I can
you know Franzi, we are too close to our Goal.
Until to-night, my Darling. May God Bless and Protect you. May
e us further, as He has in the past.
I'll be thinking of you every moment until we are to-gether again.

Yours for always,
Melvin

S.
Cie Kocham bardzo, bardzo, wiele.

The Evening of Dec. 20,1946
Ludwigsburg,Germany

arest Darling Franzi,

By the time you receive this letter,Honey,I'll be with you. We will be to-geth-
r for seventeen day,Franzi. They will be like days in heaven.

I hope this ketter finds you in the very best of health. I am feeling fine, I
ave been thinking of the many moments you and I will have with each other.

We will be to-gether for many days to come ,Franzi. You and I,and in time our
isitors,will be to-gether for the remainder of our lives. I'll always cherish and love
u as I do this day,which is more then I can express in writing. Someday,Honey,we will
able to look at our past and recall the many happy moments in which we have had each
here presence. I love you ,Franzi, I'll always love you. I wish that life wasn't so
ort. I wish that we could spend a million years on earth,you and I.

I hope you haven't worried,my Darling,I couldn't telephone you to-day. The time
ll come ,Franzi,when we won't need to worry of letters nor phone calls. We will be to-
ther always.

Please,give my love to Mom. I hope she is well. I will see both,of you to-morrow.
will be like returning home,with you and Mom there. I am hoping Mom doesen't change
r attitude toward me ,Franzi,now that the people of Berchtesgaden know of our engage-
nt. She is a very understanding person,I am sure it won't bother her any.

We will have ample time to insure Mom that we will leave her knowing that every-
ing will be well,when we leave. I want to be positive that she is well taken care of
fore we do go to America. I don't want you to worry,nor myself,that something may
ppen while we are gone. She is my mother also.

I want to assure her that I will take very good care of her wonderful daughter.
ant her to be able to trust me,Honey, that I will treat you well always. I am sure
already has that feeling.

You both are very wonderful,Franzi. I thank God that He has brought us to-gether.
y the 14th,a day for both of us to remember. I will be with you again on this day in
coming year.

Until to-morrow ,my Darling,May God Bless and Protect you every moment of your
e.

I love you very much,Franzi.

Kocham bardzo wiele.

Always yours,
Melvin

Franziska Porn
Berchtesgaden
Nonntal 14

Berchtesgaden,
20.1.~~1946~~ 1947

My darling,

One hour ago you left my dear, I feel lonely. You are going by train just now, J guess you are passing Reichenhall already. J didn't see you leaving from the Post, J am sorry, J must have missed you. - J forgot to say to you Mame love this morning, J was a little absent minded, J had each moment of this week-end in my thoughts . You are right, though it seems to be impossible, each hour more brings us together closter. My dear J think of our happiness last night , it was a great happiness we felt for the first time, J still have ants in my blood, thinking of it.
My dear J am listening to the music of the Post, it reminds me so much of our evenings we spent there. In memory J see us sitting holding hands or dancing. - J am very glad you like the same music J do, it is one step more into our understanding. Maybe we are lucky and will be able to attend the festivals this summer. But for sure we will be listening to our own symphonie, beeing at a lonely spot in God's nature, looking to the sky and moving clouds, listening to the stories and songs of forest, brooks and birds. They will remain in us like precious paintings or chapters of an novelle .

J hope you feel fine my dear and you don't have it bad at your new building.

A few nights J will be very busy at home, in writing, learning my lessons and mending clothes , J don't mind, as the time will be passing fasteer. J am already ~~the~~ counting the days till the 8 th of Februaty, there are still 18 days left. The will be filled with our thougts of past and future. Boy, ~~then~~ till then our love will be

s o o o o big .

J am looking forward to receive your call Tuesday or Wednesday.

J kiss you my dear, J am happy.

Only Yours

Francis

From the 1st of March we get new stamps!
I have to tell that my carlless boy!! Hela.
Hello from Luci

To my darling ,
Berchtesgaden
27 ~~December~~ January 1947
noon

J got a few minutes spare in the office, J want to use them to say to you hello, J am well, my love and best thank for the five letters including that from Esther. They were waiting at home like a gift. My dear, J had only the time to read them once, there was so much to read and my spare time at noon was over to fast. J am going to the theatre tonight, before J will read them over again and J can pretend to be near you the whole evening. My darling, Athough the time was short for reading, J found out, each letter contains so very sweet words. J am still smiling and s o o happy.
My dear, just now J got your call, J thankyou so much. J have given you two kisses my dear at the phone, J asked you twice if you have anderstood it . But you didnt understand nor hear it. J am sorry darling, my kiss couldn't touch your lips. J was quite alone at the office.
My dear, if you can make it, J would prefer to see you staying hear the w h o l e Sunday at your next visit, as it is the only day J can be with you.
Mam didn't accept the kiss from me, no, she wants to get it only from you, she doesn't mind whether you have a beard like a bear. But me darling, ha ha ha.
Tonight is a melody show, J will attend it with Mam and Anni together. Over the week end Anni and me were skiing. Hilda was prevented. We visited that man at the hospital and also Anni's sister. She is better now. In that room were only woumen becoming mothers. J pictured myself at a hospital, getting your daily visit, having a healthy child. J praydd and asked God for letting as beeing so happy once. But darling, J hope J have not to stay there longer then necessary, J should like to go there the last day.
My dear, J fell on my noble spot at skiing yesterday. My goodness, that was not pleasent, J fell on the mainroad and it was very hard. But we had big fun. Anni was " searching flowers" too.
In the evening we saw at the movie " Tom Dick and Harry". There, the girl went with her boyfriedd bowling, it reminded me so much of Ludwigsburg. But she was a little bit more unknowing ~~than me~~ about it then me. So J have not to be ashamed.
O darling, that would be fine, if we could go to Salzburg together this summer. Js Mac's girl not an Austrian ?
M dear J have to close now, many works are waiting for me, maybe the boss is coming too very soon, Also hello from Anni and Mr. Leidmann, they came just know, they are very pleased of your regards.
Till tomorrow J will get your call and J will be able to write in the evening - J kiss and hug you hoping to see you very soon and well.

Please, say Hello to Mam at the club, J am glad she understands our love, today she will have a reason more to smile, handing you the letter.

Only Yours
Honey.

Franzi Ponn

Berchtesgaden, den 12.2.47.

My darling,

I am sitting in the evening at home, for I was very busy this afternoon. I suppose you are going toward Ulm now, as it is 9.30 already. I hope you are well, my dear, take good care of yourself. I miss you my darling, your gentleness, smiling, caressing and even bothering. I hope to get a phone call tomorrow, as I am more rested then. I am so anxious whether the transfer will work out. We got so much to thank God, for He has answered some of our prayers already. May-be we may have it so good to be together in Berchtesgaden for the rest of our staying in Europe. One of the next days I will write to Lothar and Mam thanking for their benefit, the wonderful boxes. That from today contains (as you wanted it to know): coffee, cocoa, tea, candy, meat, thread, needles, 2 pair of stockings, panties and slip. They are very charming. That box had your Mam's address on it, I will Lotha beg to say her my heartily thank meanwhile, later I hope to be able to thank her personally. –

How is my measure man? Longing? What did Pet and Carl say about the transfer? I am sure they will be sad seeing you leaving. I hope my dear you get over here too a few real friends.
I am going to bed pretty soon today, as I feel sleepy.

Good night darling, come back soon.
Mom likes you a lot.
Good may bless you.

only Yours

Fransi.

Feb. 8, 1947
Ludwigsburg, Germany

My Dearest Darling Franzi,

I'm a sleepy little, Honey. I was going to phone you this morning, but I overslept. I'll phone you this afternoon.

Only one more day, my Darling, I'll be on my way to you. Now that I think of the past days which parted us, it seems as though the time had gone rapidly. Maybe it was because I was always thinking, dreaming, and writing, of being with you.

Before I went to bed, after I finished writing to you, I thought of you and the people in Berchtesgaden. They are very silly. [illegible] they have no hope for the future. The remarks that they made, to the girl married to an American, are like those of children.

I don't suppose we can blame them, Franzi. They are not sure of to-morrow, nor do they have something to look forward to. We have our whole life to live before us, you and I together. We have to bring new lives into this world.

I hope that the talking of the people won't hurt Mom. I'm not worrying about you in this matter, my Darling. You are young, smart, and strong. What they say you can ignore. But, we do have reason to worry about Mom. She is old, weak, and is more easily depressed. She has worked very hard for both of you. The people could take advantage of her age, illness, and past experience. I pray that that won't happen.

Please, give my love to Mom.

It is still snowing, Hon, I don't think I will be able to ski to your church. You can understand, Franzi, the snow isn't deep enough, it is too wet. And it would take too long. Boy! am I filled with desire to-day.

The words of your beautiful letter, which I received yesterday, still linger in my mind. It was a very precious letter, my Darling. It is one which I will endeavor never to lose. It tells me what a wonderful wife you will be.

I'm smoking my pipe while writing you this letter. I wish there would be a way for me to [illegible] fragrant smoke. But, I wish to be with you when you receive this letter.

I'm very glad I'll have 5 days with you, Hon. We have many things to discuss. I'm sure you, the Mom, want to speak of things that concern us. I wish that I could speak [illegible] German so that I could tell Mom the many things that I know she would want to hear. She can be sure that I'll always love you and protect you. I'll do everything in my power to make you happy. I'll do everything possible to prove that I am worthy of such a wonderful wife as you. I know I am lucky, Hon. To me, you are the perfect woman.

Already it is mid-morning. In a few hours, I will be hearing your wonderful voice. Then, the remainder of the day will go very fast. To-morrow morning, I will phone you once again. To assure you that everything is in order, that I will be leaving in the afternoon on my journey to you.

Anni will be smiling and watching you, assuring you that everything will be alright. I will reach you safely. I will have a wide smile on my lips, thanking God for helping me to get the opportunity to be with you again, praying I will get my [illegible].

Until this afternoon, when I hear you over the phone. May God be with you. I'll always love you, my Darling.

Faithfully yours forever,

Melvin

P.S.
Ich Liebe Dich.

The Evening of Feb. 17, 1947
Ludwigsburg, Germany

To my dearly beloved.

My Dearest Darling Franzi,

I had the sound of your sweet voice lingering with me through the entire day, Honey. You sounded sleepy, Franzi.

By the time you receive this letter, Honey, I'll be in Berchtesgaden. For a long time, I'll be there to stay.

I phoned our Headquarters about the transfer to-day. They said that the papers are already made out. We will receive them to-morrow morning. We will leave Wednesday morning for Berchtesgaden. God has answered our prayers, my Darling. We can thank Him Sunday, when you and I will go to church to-gether.

I won't have to worry that perhaps something can happen to you or Mom. I will be there each day, to protect you.

I received your wonderful letter from last Wednesday, Franzi. Your words are still in my mind.

I will be expecting your letter from Friday, to-morrow. If you wrote one, did you?

To-morrow, I will phone you in the morning to give you the good news. It was too late to phone you to-day, Honey. I received the information myself at a few minutes past 5 o'clock. You weren't working then.

We can do all of the things that we planned, Honey. We can go walking, skiing, swimming, and do so many other things that will bring us [illegible] closer to-gether, and make us happier.

Please, give Mom my love, Franzi. I hope she never tires of me, Hon. We will be seeing a lot of each other.

I must remember to tell you to wait-up for me on Wednesday, Honey. I'll tell you over the phone to-morrow, if I don't forget.

I'll be able to hear your sweet voice only in the day again. The remainder of the day will go rapidly.

I'll also be very busy to-morrow. I have many things to do. I will have to prepare for my leaving.

People in Berchtesgaden will be able to see us to-gether almost every day. No matter what they say, my Darling, we will take it in stride.

I'm glad that spring is here, Honey. We will be able to go walking, to visit the same places that we did last year.

Two of the fellows here had their marriages approved, Franzi. They only have to wait a little longer. Perhaps, if we are lucky, Honey, and God will be with us, we may be able to be married in Berchtesgaden.

To-night, to-morrow night, and then Wednesday night. Only 3 days then I'll be with you.

Until to-morrow, my Darling. May God be with you

Good-night, Sweetheart.

Yours forever,

Melvin

P.S.

Ich Liebe Dich.

Chapter Eleven
Christmas in Berchtesgaden (1946)

Little did I realize the dramatic events about to take place during my leave in Berchtesgaden in December, 1946. My departure from Ludwigsburg and the 633rd Medical Clearing Company was made easier by the knowledge that I would soon be with Frances in Berchtesgaden for two full weeks. All of my original friends of the 633rd Medical Clearing Company who were draftees were gone. No doubt all were back home in the United States by January 1, 1947. Many would probably take advantage of the G.I. Bill of Rights and attend college. A few of the men would decide to make the Army their careers. Several would return to civilian careers that had been interrupted by the draft and World War II. Some would find it very difficult to adjust to civilian life after their Army tours. But, they were back home in the land of the round door knobs and the world's biggest PX. Their replacements were all regular Army. After saying good-bye to Jim, I picked up my travel bags and walked to the Ludwigsburg train station for the trip to Berchtesgaden and Frances. The snow was falling. Winter was evident.

I transferred in Stuttgart to a train destined for Munich. In Munich I would then transfer for the last leg of the trip to Berchtesgaden. The long journey provided ample time to reminisce and to wonder what the future would bring for Frances and I. It appeared as though the train was barely moving. Time seemed to pass too slowly. The train always seemed to crawl on

the trip to Berchtesgaden. The reverse was true on my return to Ludwigsburg. I was eager to see Frances and to spend the Christmas Holidays in Berchtesgaden. As the train passed the Munich suburbs, it was possible to see the snow capped Bavarian Alps in the distance. It was a beautiful scene. The fields and towns along the way were all covered with snow. I had no doubt that I would find the Watzmann, the Jenner, and other mountains surrounding the valley of Berchtesgaden covered with a winter blanket of snow. My arrival on the 23rd of December was totally in accord with my expectations. Fortunately the sun was shining and the weather was clear. I was "home" for the Holidays.

Immediately after visiting the Army's billeting office and checking into the Bellevue Hotel, I went to visit Fran and her mother. I was not able to contact Frances prior to leaving Ludwigsburg. Hence, she had no idea of my status or location. I knocked on her door and waited. The apartment door opened and there stood my Frances. Apparently she was home for lunch. She threw open the door and jumped into my arms, sobbing, telling me she was worried because she did not know what was happening. After a few moments she settled down and I took the opportunity to apologize for not contacting her prior to leaving Ludwigsburg. After hugging and kissing in the doorway, we finally came to our senses and we entered the apartment together. Her mom was just as surprised. I mentioned to Fran that I had two full weeks to spend with her. This time would extend into the first part of 1947. She returned to her office at the newspaper and I returned to the Bellevue Hotel to shower,

shave, and go shopping at the local Army PX for Christmas presents. I was able to purchase French perfume for Frances and a set of beautiful dessert plates that were the product of Czechoslovakia for her mother.

I could not get over the beauty of the Alps in the winter time. Fortunately my hotel room faced the valley and some of the mountains surrounding the town. I could see the Goll, Brett, Kehlstein, and Obersalzburg. They were all covered with snow. It was only the second time in my life I was able to see any mountains in the winter time. Oberjoch was the first occasion and that was a distant memory.

The first evening together I gave Fran a complete review of my actions to try to remain in Germany, including my enlistment in the Army. At this stage, there were many unknowns relating to the Army's wedding ban. The rumors still persisted that the ban would be dropped soon. However, no one had any idea of the time element. Fran and I concentrated on planning how to spend my two weeks leave. We would account for every day and evening.

We decided to spend most of our time taking short walks. It was too cold to venture out to distant places. The weather was clear, cold but sunny. It was perfect for skiing or winter sports and excellent for taking short walking trips near and around the town of Berchtesgaden. It was perfect weather for the Holidays. We planned on attending Midnight Mass at one of the two local Catholic Churches, the Franciscan Church. The local cemetery was adjacent to the church. We planned on stopping at the

cemetery prior to attending Mass. Frances' mother had lost two baby daughters in child birth. She also lost a son due to rickets after Frances was born. They were buried in the local cemetery adjacent to the Church.

Christmas Eve was very special for us and particularly for me. I reminisced about the many Christmas Eves I had spent in Toledo. It was a special time for the family to have a reunion at my parents' home. After exchanging Christmas presents we would attend St. Anthony's Catholic Church to celebrate Midnight Mass. But on Christmas Eve, 1946, I would be with Frances and her mother in Berchtesgaden. This too, would be an event I would never forget. It was the first of many Christmases we would share. I remember the event as though it was yesterday. After sharing Christmas cookies, we prepared to go to church. I was shocked to see Fran's mother bring a live Christmas tree into the apartment. She proceeded to place candles on the tree. To my amazement she lit the candles. I had never seen a Christmas tree with live candles. Certainly the fire hazard was evident. She paid no mind to the possibility of a fire. I learned that this was the custom in Germany, i.e., to use live candles on the Christmas tree. To my relief, Fran's mom extinguished the candles as we prepared to go to church. Again to my amazement, Fran's mom picked up the tree to take to church. I could never imagine what was coming next. The night was cold. There must have been several feet of snow on the ground and it was still snowing as we departed for the midnight Mass. We could hear the snow crunching under our feet as we walked along the way.

It was only a short walk from the apartment to the cemetery and church. Fran tried to explain to me what was going on but I was too involved in just observing the developing events. We entered the cemetery where Fran's siblings were buried, two baby girls and one two year old baby boy. Fran's mom placed the Christmas tree into the snow on the grave site and lit the candles. I was really astonished at this action especially when Fran and her mother proceeded to walk away from the tree with the lit candles and toward the church. Fran assured me that there was no danger of a fire. There was too much snow on the ground. The tree was fresh and hence not flammable. Fran assured me that it was a local custom on Christmas Eve and no one had ever had any bad experiences. It was no surprise to Fran and her mom that even when the candles had burned down totally there was no fire. I can't say that I felt the same.

The cemetery was a beautiful site. There were many Christmas trees with lit candles on most of the grave sites. It truly was a remarkable way to celebrate Christmas Eve. But the night was not over. In keeping with tradition from many years past, the night silence was broken by the sounds of the special blunderbuss guns being fired in the mountains surrounding Berchtesgaden. The discharge of these special weapons containing blanks continued during the midnight Mass and ended about one o'clock on Christmas morning. The local farmers retained this tradition. The noise from the guns, they sounded similar to the Army's 105 mm artillery guns, echoed throughout the valley.

Obviously, the men had synchronized their watches. The weapons were fired in sequence from one mountain to another until the entire perimeter of the valley was covered. Any visitors to Berchtesgaden had to be impressed by the various traditional Christmas events. It was an evening to remember.

Fran's mother invited me to dinner for Christmas Day. I felt guilty. I knew that food was scarce but both Fran and her mom insisted that I have dinner with them. I did acquiesce knowing all of the time that I would limit what I would eat. I planned and did have a meal at the Army dining room in the Bellevue Hotel prior to going to their home. I limited the amount of food I ate in order to leave some room for the "next" dinner. I was pleasantly surprised by the meal prepared by Fran's mom. It was a typical Bavarian meal of "kaiserschmann". It was, in my view, a sort of pancake mix chopped up into bite size pieces and covered lightly with sugar. It was very tasty. I was glad I accepted the dinner invitation.

After Christmas, Fran and I went walking. While she worked, I went skiing at the Skytop Hotel, also managed and operated by and for American military personnel. The days were cold and sunny. It was invigorating being outdoors. On week-ends, Fran and her mom took me to visit relatives and friends. One of the visits was to Fran's uncle on a farm located in Unterau, a settlement on Obersalzburg. It was unusual to say the least. The heating system was a ceramic stove in the corner of the living room and kitchen area. Her uncle had a few laughs when I mentioned that I had seen a similar heating system on display

in the Toledo Art Museum. Fran had her hands full translating between her uncle, aunt, cousin, her mother, and me. At times, Fran became confused and addressed me in German and her uncle in English. But everything turned out fine. We all had many laughs. The family did accept me which made Fran and I very happy.

On one of my free days, I visited the local U.S. Army dispensary in town. I thought that I might inquire about a possible transfer from the 633rd Medical Clearing Company to Berchtesgaden. To my surprise, the medical officer in charge (OIC), who happened to be a native of Cleveland, Ohio, indicated that he would try to arrange the transfer. He stated that they were short of help. I told him that I had no medical training but was eager to learn enough to be of some assistance to him and his staff. He asked me why I wanted to transfer to Berchtesgaden. I was honest and told him that I wanted to marry a lady in Berchtesgaden. He told me that he would try to have me transferred to Bechtesgaden. Frankly, I did not have too much hope for success.

To my surprise, and to the surprise of hundreds of American military service men in Germany, the Stars and Stripes, the Army's unofficial newspaper, published on January 1, 1947, indicated that the Army was lifting both the non-fraternization and wedding bans between American and Germans. This was very big news. I told Fran that we would start immediately on preparing the paper work. There was a great deal of paper work and bureaucracy to overcome. The requirements for obtaining approval for the American and German couples to marry were

also published in the Stars and Stripes. The list was long. The couple would have to be interviewed by an Army Chaplain plus the soldier's Commanding Officer. Approval from both was required. The soldier would have to have at least six months remaining in the European Theater of Operations(Germany). If the soldier was not 21 years of age, he would need the written consent to the marriage from his parents/guardians. If the marriage was approved by the Army, the soldier would have to be out of the European Theater within 30 days after the marriage. He would have to sign a document that he would never return to Germany. The German lady would have to complete a "fragebogan/questionnaire" detailing her entire life including a special police report that every German civilian had on file at the local police station. All of this documentation was required to be submitted through channels to higher Headquarters for final approval or disapproval of the marriage.

If the Army approved the marriage, the couple would be allowed to spend seven days at any U.S. Army recreation area, free of charge. The couple would be given a thirty day window in which to have the marriage take place. If the thirty day window was missed, the approval was withdrawn. After the marriage, the couple could not live in Army quarters. The soldier was not permitted to live on the economy. The requirements posed a challenge to the couple and the Army.

Frances and I began to digest the Army's list of requirements and made plans to start our paper work immediately. Prior to departing Berchtesgaden for Ludwigsburg after a beautiful

Christmas vacation with Frances, we both knew that we would need patience, luck, and God's help in accomplishing our objective. But, there was light at the end of the tunnel. I departed from Berchtesgaden hopeful that the year 1947 would be good to Fran and I.

There were many unknowns that had to be faced. What would be the final requirements of the Army for American military personnel to marry German nationals? Would the various officials approve our request to marry? How would Fran and I get to the United States, i.e., would we travel together from Germany to Toledo or would we travel separately? Where would we live in Germany after our marriage until I would be ordered to leave Germany? Where would we live in Ohio? Would I attend Toledo University under the G.I. Bill of Rights? The questions seemed to be endless with few, if any, answers forthcoming. But, the first and biggest hurdle was behind us, i.e., the lifting of the wedding ban. It was just a question of time, patience, and hope.

Chapter Twelve
My Last Days in Ludwigsburg

My return to Ludwigsburg in early January, 1947, after the Christmas and New Year's Holidays in Berchtesgaden was a very difficult period. I had to become adjusted to the routines of regular Army life, if one could call it that. After two weeks of being with Frances enjoying sledding and skiing plus taking many walks in the area, this was the most trying time of my entire stay in Ludwigsburg. There was however the extremely bright news relating to the United States Army lifting both the non-fraternization and wedding bans between American military personnel and Germans. The latter was certainly the best news not only for Fran and I but for countless other American and German couples who were also waiting for this good news. I never did pay attention to the non-fraternization ban. It had outlived its purpose. It was obviously intended to prevent close relationships from developing at the end of WW II between the United States military personnel and German civilian men, women, and even children. The ban was obviously political in nature. The wedding ban was also, in my opinion, politically motivated.

Rescinding the bans was obviously the sensible thing to do. Be that as it may, rescinding the bans made life more acceptable for everyone in Germany. My objective was to start gathering information for the preparation of the vast amount of documentation that would be required to marry Frances.

I assumed my new duties as acting Mess Sergeant. But, with all of the help in the Army mess hall, I had no worries. I returned to the business of writing letters to Frances and making phone calls to her office. In order to reach Frances via the telephone, I still had to use both the Army and German civilian lines. Making a phone call in Germany via the civilian lines continued to be a fantastic and challenging experience. Just getting through was difficult enough and not the end of the ordeal. Maintaining the open line without being pre-empted by the Army or being disconnected accidentally was difficult. I was able to ascertain that Fran was still having difficulties obtaining information on visas from the civilian authorities and the appointed American Military Governor(MG). It was obvious that both offices and their personnel were still not enamored with the idea of a German marrying an American and vise versa.

It was very understandable that many Germans would have a difficult time accepting the idea of one of their own marrying an "Ami", as the Americans were often referred to by the Germans. The name Ami was used by the majority of Germans in their day to day conversations in discussing American military personnel in Germany. Unfortunately many American military personnel did not enjoy seeing their fellow Americans contemplating marriage with a former enemy. Accordingly, both the American and German planning on marrying were bound to be ostracized by many of their fellow countrymen. It was, however, a true test of family and friends. Fortunately both Frances and I had close relationships with our families. We soon learned the identities of

our true friends. In my case, my family in Toledo was surprised when I told them of my engagement to marry Frances. But they did support me without any reservations and in fact, they were enthusiastic in their letters to me. They requested pictures of Frances and asked questions about Berchtesgaden, how we met, and when we might be coming to Toledo. This was welcomed news. I never did indicate to my family that I was willing to stay in Germany to marry Fran even if it required me to stay as a civilian. Fortunately, the situation never called for this alternative.

I was never able to say the same for many of the men in my Company. Some were hostile. Their remarks left no doubt in my mind that they strongly opposed any serious relationships between American military personnel and German women. A small group of about five men offered me congratulations and even asked if there was anything that they could do to assist me in any way. It was a great gesture on their part and I thanked them for their offer. But, there was absolutely nothing that they could do to help. It was all in the hands of the Army.

Considering the distance between Berchtesgaden and Ludwigsburg, it was inevitable that the preparation of the necessary documentation for marriage would be challenging. The requirements to be interviewed by my Commanding Officer and an Army Chaplain under the present geographical separation would pose a major problem. However, the interviews were part of the requirements established by the Army. I decided to visit Berchtesgaden with the intention of once again visiting the office

of the American Military Governor, MG, assigned to the town. My objective was to obtain whatever support he could provide. Again, Jim made certain that I would be given leave to visit Berchtesgaden. His leave policy continued to facilitate my many visits and was extremely considerate. I thanked him profusely for his actions.

I arrived in Berchtesgaden and had a beautiful reunion with Fran and her mother. As always, I stayed at the Bellevue Hotel. Fran and I took our usual walks to several of our favorite sites in the Berchtesgaden area. A visit to the Maria Gern church was number one on our list of places to visit. Visiting the church served several purposes. It gave us an opportunity to not only say a prayer in this historic church but to view the beautiful art within. Standing outside of the entrance to the church it is possible to view the Watzmann mountain and the local farms located across the valley. The walk from the town is in itself a wonderful experience. A person becomes captured by the beauty of the surrounding mountains and countryside. Another favored walk that was always on our agenda was following the river to Koenigsee. Ironically, we encountered few people on this walk. We had taken this walk many times, never tiring of the beauty of the river and the view of the mountains that could be seen from the path.

After spending the week-end with Frances, I returned to Ludwigsburg with the normal sadness. It was difficult to imagine a bright future for Frances and I. The problems appeared to be astronomical. But, we would continue to press for solutions to

our goal to marry. My return to my military duties took on a new perspective. While I was in Berchtesgaden, the Company received a qualified Mess Sergeant. He requested that I stay on the job and to continue with all of functions as usual. He was an Army trained cook and a Technical Sergeant, several levels above my grade of T/4, the equivalent of a Sergeant. He did have one major problem, this was his first assignment in Germany. He had no knowledge of the language, customs, and local national (LN) rules that governed the civilian employees. The big surprise to him was the fact that all LN's, German and displaced persons, were to receive one full meal a day as part of their benefits. This was the true motive for all LN's to work for the American military forces in Germany. Food was scarce on the economy. Many people were starving due to the war and the breakdown of the markets and distribution system. I did not mind the work relationship. The new Mess Sergeant was very considerate and certainly generous in continued to permit me to visit Berchtesgaden every week-end. I was still able to leave Ludwigsburg on Friday and, after spending the week-end in Berchtesgaden, return to my home base on Monday. We were both very happy in our positions.

Once again in January, 1947, I visited with Frances and we both reviewed our progress in preparing documentation. It seemed an impossible task. I was committed to the Army for one year. We needed a miracle to help solve our dilemma. It came suddenly and occured after I returned to Ludwigsburg.

During the last week of January, 1947, Jim came into the mess hall and asked if I was ready for some real good news. I could not imagine what the news could be. Jim told me that the Company had received orders from Bad Tolz, Germany, transferring me to Berchtesgaden. I was pleasantly stunned. The news was just too good to be true. I had to pinch myself to make certain that it was real. This was the very best news possible. It meant that I would be transferred to Berchtesgaden, be close to Frances, and we would be in a position to prepare the necessary paper work demanded by the United States Army for their approval of our marriage. After the initial shock wore off and thanking Jim for the news, I phoned Frances at her office and passed on the information. I advised her that it would take a few days to have the necessary paper work cleared in the Company and for me to pack my belongings. These actions would take a short time and I would soon be on my way to my new military post in Berchtesgaden. The miracle we prayed for had happened.

I did have some sad feelings in preparing to leave the 633rd Medical Clearing Company and the many good experiences I enjoyed during my assignment. There was no question in my mind that I was very fortunate that the Army assigned me to an organization that was more like a civilian environment than a military unit. Given the fact that I had no medical, administrative, or even clerical training, it was very unusual to be assigned to an Army medical Army unit. But, for the assignment to manage a hospital in a prisoner of war camp it was not necessary to have a medical background. However, it would have helped to

understand the needs of the medical staff. It would also have been helpful if I had administrative training or experience. I had neither. Hence, my work assignment in the Company was very unusual to put it mildly. No doubt this was due to the lack of experienced Army personnel caused by the rapid deployment of the United States armed forces from Europe immediately following the end of hostilities in Germany.

I enjoyed the company of the men who served with me. We were all from different parts of the United States and represented various ethnic groups. The Army was segregated at the time. It was ironic. We had American Indians and Hispanic troops in the Army serving with white troops. Black men and women served in separate Army units. The Army was integrated after WW II by President Truman in 1947.

As the Company's athletic director, I was responsible for organizing various sports activities. I really enjoyed organizing the intramural softball games. This brought the entire Company of men closer together. After the games we enjoyed getting together at the Stuttgarter Tor, the club established by the Company Commander. It was a time in the evenings when the men could relax and enjoy a coca cola or Dinkel Acker beer and maybe dance with Polish, Hungarian, German or other ladies who visited the club regularly.

Probably the one item that not only I but all of the men in the Company would miss were the many discussions we had relating to politics, ambitions, objectives in life, and many other serious matters. This was a period in all of our lives that we would

always remember. We were very fortunate to be in a military organization that had a very special mission and was small enough that the men could develop close relationships. Living in private quarters was certainly a tremendous luxury that few military personnel could hope to enjoy during their military tour in Germany in 1945 and immediate postwar years. Every member of the Company lived in private quarters in the spring of 1945, when it assumed its peacetime mission, through 1946. The civilian quarters were seized by the Army from German civilians who were known members of the NAZI party during the war. The Army ordered the German owners to vacate the housing immediately and without any of the furnishings except for bedding. The Germans had to fend for themselves. Due to the political changes taking place in Europe and due to the cold war, the private housing confiscated from the Germans would be returned to the Germans.

My last days in the 633rd Medical Clearing Company and Ludwigsburg passed rapidly. After saying farewell to Jim and the others in the Company, I departed for Berchtesgaden at the end of January, 1947. This would turn out to be my last train ride from Ludwigsburg to Berchtesgaden while serving in the Army. I never imagined that I would visit Ludwigsburg nearly fifty years later in 1994 and retrace my steps in the "former" housing area, our Company Headquarters, and the Stuttgarter Tor. I would also find, of course, that Camp 78, located in Zuffenhausen, Germany, would be gone. In place, the German Government had built a public park and garden.

Part V

Chapter Thirteen
Assignment Berchtesgaden

Being assigned to the Bavarian garden spot, Berchtesgaden, was difficult to grasp. I arrived via train in mid-afternoon in late January, 1947. My arrival was greeted with a beautiful day. The sun was shining brightly. The weather was crystal clear. It was a typical cold winter day in the Alps. The top of the Watzmann and other mountains surrounding the town were covered with snow that made the mountains glisten in the bright sunlight. I reminisced of my first weekend in Berchtesgaden and my amazement at the beauty of the Alps surrounding the city. There was no way I could have ever imagined having a duty station in Berchtesgaden and the surrounding area. But here I was in a land that I would never have hoped to see, let alone, be assigned to for Army duty way back in May, 1945, when I volunteered for my immediate induction into the Army.

My first action was to report to the medical dispensary and to the Captain who was responsible for having me transferred to Berchtesgaden. I thanked him profusely for his action. He proceeded to advise me to proceed to my assigned quarters located in a small compound just outside of the city and on the road to the beautiful Koenigsee. He also was very considerate and told me take two days off to get organized and to advise Frances of my assignment and arrival. I will always be indebted to the Captain from Youngstown, Ohio. He introduced me to all of the staff, approximately ten people, and advised me that

I would be working with two of the trained enlisted medical technicians. They would assist me in learning some of the basic first aid measures. I knew that I was very fortunate indeed.

After checking into the Alpine Inn, yes, that is where my private room was located, I immediately walked into town to visit Frances at her office. She could hardly believe that we would be together. No more week-end visits. We would have time to visit various scenic parts of the area, her relatives, and friends. Most important, we would be able to start our paperwork to have the Army approve our marriage. My assignment to Berchtesgaden would facilitate very close coordination in preparing the necessary documentation to satisfy the demands established by the Army. The submission of the data would also be simplified due to our location in the same town.

One of the first actions Fran and I did was to prepare a list of the various documents the Army required to obtain approval of the American/German marriage. We already knew that we needed to be interviewed and the marriage approved by my Commanding Officer and an Army Chaplain (of any denomination). We believed these actions could be scheduled immediately. There were no special forms to be completed. Letters recommending approval of our marriage would be required from my Commanding Officer and the Army Chaplain. The coming days would be filled with activities from morning to night, Fran at the newspaper office and me at the dispensary. After the normal work day Fran and I would be able to take a short walk around the town. We were able to schedule the

interviews in a matter of days. Both the Commanding Officer and the Chaplain approved our marriage.

The questions of both men were somewhat similar. They asked our ages, how we met, did our families approve of the marriage, what were our future plans and expectations in life. Both men also asked me what my objectives were in respect to supporting Frances. My response to this question probably was the most thought provoking of all. I knew that I wanted to attend college. Even although I had a technical skill, albeit limited, in machine shop operations, I knew that I wanted to become involved in industrial management. I also knew that this would not be an easy task considering that I would have to have an income to support Fran. Fran and I had discussed our future many times including my plans after my return to civilian life. Hence, my response was consistent with our discussions many weeks and months prior to this interview. I indicated that I had planned to attend college and concurrently find part time employment in order to support Fran. As we learned later in Toledo, tens of thousands of American WW II veterans followed the same courses of action after they too were discharged from the military services. At this time, neither Fran nor I had given any thought to Fran going to work in the United States. Both officers reminded me that they respected my response but cautioned me that I should be prepared to make personal sacrifices along our journey. They were impressed with the fact that Fran and I had already discussed our plans in advance. They were convinced we were very serious people. Of course, they asked what our plans

were for starting a family. Fran and I had planned on having children after we were settled in the United States and I was in position to provide for a family. Both the Army Chaplain and my Commanding Officer provided strong letters approving our union. Fran and I were very grateful for their actions. There was no doubt in our minds that their letters and recommendations approving our marriage would provide strong justification for the Army's approval at the next higher Army Headquarters of our application to marry.

I was required to sign a statement that I would never return to Germany if my request to marry a German was approved. This requirement was no doubt in consideration of the timing, i.e., very shortly after hostilities ended and prior to the "cold war" between the United States and Russia. It was also interesting that no such statement was required of an American military person wanting to marry any other foreign national, for example, Polish, Hungarian, Italian, Belgium or other European including a Russian displaced person. My statement would accompany all of the documentation required by the Army. I had no problem with signing this letter. Years later, with the "cold war" developments between the United States and Russia, this United States policy was discarded. Thousands of American service men and also Department of Defense civilians would return for duty and employment in Germany together with their former German war brides and families.

Frances was required to complete a lengthy questionnaire relating to her total background, including the history of her

parents. No doubt the latter was to ascertain if her parents were active in the NAZI party. Since all Germans were required by German law to be registered with the local Police, Fran also had to have a report from the German police showing no record of criminal actions. Of course, if there was any recorded criminal action, it would be reflected on the report. The report was clear and was subsequently forwarded with the application for marriage in April, 1946, to higher Headquarters, located in Bad Tolz, Germany. We never did learn the "next higher" Army echelons our request for marriage was submitted to for final action, i.e., for approval or disapproval. In any case, the die was cast. We no longer were in control of our destiny. Now our future was in the hands of the United States Army.

We submitted all of the necessary documentation and waited patiently for the Army's approval of our request to marry. In the interim we would be busy at our mutual work stations. I was occupied in the Army dispensary. Fran was very busy working for the newspaper. Ironically, this activity was excellent for Fran. She had to communicate with the Americans requesting printing support from the newspaper. The paper printed church programs for various denominations, bulletins for various Army offices, chit books for use by American personnel for purchasing food and refreshments in the Army operated hotels, and other Army miscellaneous printing needs. These actions improved her English language capabilities tremendously.

The waiting period also gave Fran and I the week-ends to spend visiting the many various beautiful and interesting

places surrounding the area of Berchtesgaden. We took many walks to the local villages. Unterau was a short distance from the center of Berchtesgaden. The area was pristine. The traffic was practically non-existent in 1946 and 1947. The German population was still recuperating from the war years. Civilian transportation was restricted to public transportation and bicycles. The surrounding fields of the village were covered with wild flowers and stretches of forests in the background. The area was, and still is, a paradise for artists from all over the world. The very pleasant problem of the artist was trying to decide which scene to capture on canvas.

We always had a great pleasure in visiting the village of Ramsau. The walk in itself was breath taking. One could view the mountains from various angles. Ramsau has probably one of the most photographed churches in Germany. The scene with the church in the background in any season of the year is truly spectacular. At the time of our first visit in the spring of 1947, the view was amazing. A small river carrying the water from Hintersee, an Alpine lake within walking distance of Ramsau, flows swiftly through the center of the village. The mountains surrounding the town remind many visitors of the Dolomite Alps in Italy. One of our most memorable visits to Ramsau involved Fran and I riding bicycles from her home in Berchtesgaden to Ramsau. Fran used her mother's bicycle and I was able to borrow a bicycle from one of Fran's close girl friends. It was daring on my part. I was not in uniform. I did not wear my Army cap. I had no tie and wore a red scarf around my neck

plus I rode a bicycle. We were never stopped by the military police (MP). Of course due to my playing softball with all of the Americans stationed in Berchtesgaden including the military police, I threw all caution aside and enjoyed the trip without any concern as to proper Army dress codes. The day was perfect for touring Ramsau.

One of the more interesting visits we made was to Ilsank, the very small area just on the outskirts of Berchtesgaden. Fran showed me where she and her parents once lived and the one room school house she attended for the first four grades prior to the family moving into the city of Berchtesgaden. She was in a classroom that also contained children of higher grades. It was a local school that accommodated the children in the immediate vicinity.

Fran also took me on a day's walk to visit her aunt and uncle on the farm in Scheffau, a small settlement located not too distant from Obersalzberg. We walked from Berchtesgaden to Schellenberg, a small town in the valley and on the main road leading to Salzburg, Austria. From Schellenberg we walked to the farm. It was a going to be a long day. The farm was only approximately 200 meters from the border of Austria. We always enjoyed our special visits with her aunt and uncle. No doubt both were very comfortable on the farm and with their status in life. I had no doubt that they would be totally lost if they would have to abandon the farm for any reason. Visiting Berchtesgaden or Salzburg, Austria, was something special. Such visits were very infrequent. Special holidays and related celebrations would

entice them to make visits. Fran's uncle was very interested in life in the United States. He could not grasp the fact that one State, Texas, was as large in area as Germany. The question of transportation was raised. I was able to describe the importance of train travel and the necessity for automobiles. Air travel was still limited at that time. He had many questions about farming in the United States. Being a "city boy", I was unable to describe farm operations and the various crops grown in the country. I was able to tell him about some crops grown on farms in the Toledo area, such as tomatoes, sweet corn, and potatoes. I was very happy that the family accepted me into their circle. Our walk back to Berchtesgaden made it a long, tiring but enjoyable day. We discussed the farm and the fact that her aunt and uncle were comfortably settled.

Fran and I spent some time visiting the homes of her girl friends. On the surface, I was accepted. I was certain that many wondered if my intentions were honorable. No doubt some wondered if Fran and I would marry and, if we did, would the marriage last. I had no doubts that the same reservations were in the minds of some members of my family and even my closest friends in Toledo, Ohio. No doubt the Army wanted to discourage the marriages between Americans and Germans. It was understandable at the time. WW II memories were still fresh in everyone's mind. The relations between the United States and Russia were still not clearly delineated as they would be in the near future. Germany was still considered the enemy by many Americans.

We again visited Fran's cousins on their farm located in a small village named Scheffau. We also walked to Bishofswiesen and to Oberau. Two very beautiful walks that could only be appreciated on bright, sunny days. If the weather did not permit being outdoors, it does rain often in Bavaria and that is why the fields are so green and lush looking, it provided an opportunity for me to give an orientation to Fran on life in America. It also provided us an opportunity to plan for the future. True, there were very many unknowns. But, we at least were able to develop some semblance of what I would do about attending college under the G.I. Bill of Rights, finding employment either part or full time based on the circumstances, family planning, and other key factors. We also had many unknowns relative to what the Army would or would not do even after we received permission to marry. It was unthinkable that the Army would disapprove of our marriage. I had resolved myself to a course of action if the Army did not give us approval to marry. I would remain in Germany either in the Army or as a civilian. There was no way I was going to leave Frances behind. My thoughts on the subject were crystal clear. The major question I had if the Army approved our marriage was whether we would travel to the United States together after the marriage or would I be sent home and the Army would send Frances after me? We had no idea of what actions would be taken by the Army in this matter.

Frances and I waited anxiously for news from the Army on our request to marry. We knew that when the news arrived,

we would have to initiate many critical actions in preparation for the marriage. The most sensitive action would be to advise Fran's mother. Fran was the only surviving child. Fran and her mother were extremely close. We had no idea what the future would hold or permit concerning their meeting in the future. There were many unanswered questions. Would the international situation permit future communications between the United States and Germany? Would Fran and her mom ever see each other after Fran departed for the United States? How secure would Fran's mother be in Berchtesgaden? These were only some of the immediate thoughts that came to the minds of both Fran and I. Family concerns had top priority. There were other actions that needed to be taken. Arrangements for a civil marriage was key. Germany did not recognize a church wedding. It still adheres to the same policy. I needed to contact an Army Catholic Chaplain to arrange for a church wedding and to record the marriage in both the Catholic Church and the United States Army. Of course, the civil ceremony would be recorded for centuries.

We also had no idea how we would arrange a wedding reception. Our living arrangements after our honeymoon were in question. Where would we go for a "honeymoon"? To whom would we send invitations to our marriage, e.g., my family and friends in Toledo? We certainly could not expect any of them to attend. Where would we live in Toledo? There seemed to be no end to the many questions that would have to be addressed if and when we received the word from the Army approving the

marriage of Frances, a German, to Melvin, the Ami. But, time and good fortune would answer almost all of these questions favorably.

Chapter Fourteen
Finally, The Good News

I received the Army's approval to marry Frances in late May, 1947. The news came unexpectedly. Although Frances and I prayed every day that the Army would approve our request to marry, the news did catch us off guard. It was a day to celebrate. The approval was granted with several caveats but also some outstanding aspects. One of the caveats was that we had a time limit to get married. We had a thirty day window to have the marriage take place. The Army established August 24, 1947, as the beginning of the thirty day period. If the wedding did not take place within that thirty day period, the approval was automatically canceled. August 24 in 1947 was a Sunday. The German civilian government offices were closed on Sundays and Holidays. We wanted to be married by the German civilian Government authority and, on the same day, be married by a Catholic Chaplain in the local Catholic Church. Hence, we elected to have both ceremonies take place on Monday, August 25, 1947. After the Burgermeister/Mayor married us at 9 A.M. in his office, we were married in the Stifts Catholic Church at 9:30 A.M. by a Catholic Chaplain who was stationed in Salzburg, Austria. The Chaplain made a special trip to Berchtesgaden to perform the wedding ceremony.

A second major caveat was that we were to be out of the European Theater of Operations within thirty days of our marriage. No doubt this was due in part to political reasons and

to avoid potential "in-law" problems. The collapse of the German economy, the lack of food and the day to day demands for life's necessities could place tremendous obligations on the American. In addition, I was not to live in civilian quarters and Fran was not allowed to live in United States Army housing. In 1945 and 1946 the Army had requisitioned German civilian housing, that was not destroyed by the war for use of Army military family personnel. Since the nation was still in ruins, housing on the local economy was in very short supply. It would be years until the construction boom would take place in Germany, including family housing.

There was some good news that came with the marriage approval. We were permitted to have a seven day honeymoon at any Army recreation area courtesy of the United States Army. This meant at no charge to the individual. We selected Chiemsee for our honeymoon. It was only an hour's drive from Berchtesgaden. It is the largest inland lake in Germany, located between Munich and Salzburg, Austria. The setting is outstanding. There was no indication of travel arrangements for the married couple to the United States. This seemed to be a wide open question but not too troubling for Fran and I. We speculated that the most important item was receiving the Army's approval to marry. How and when we traveled was secondary. It was only a matter of time until we would be together in Toledo. The wheels were in motion.

Due to the nature of the small contingent of military personnel stationed in Berchtesgaden, all of the personnel came in contact

with each other almost daily. Many knew Frances from the publication requirements they ordered from the newspaper. In addition, many had seen and met Fran and I on Saturday evenings at the Post Hotel where we gathered for dancing. These contact's helped Fran and I to have not seven but thirteen days on our honeymoon, ten days at Chiemsee and three days on Predigstuhl in nearby Bad Reichenhall. We were also allowed to stay at the Post Hotel after we returned from our "long" honeymoon. I was told that this would stand until we received our travel orders to Toledo. These were benefits I never expected from friends. I did send wedding invitations to my family and friends in Toledo. Of course, I knew that none could make the trip. But, I believed it to be the right thing to do. I learned later upon returning to Toledo that my family and friends did appreciate the gesture. As expected, none could attend the ceremony.

Frances advised the owner of the newspaper that she would resign as soon as we received the Army approval to marry. He appreciated the notice. There was no doubt that he felt sorry that Fran would be leaving. He and his wife treated Fran as their daughter. I had developed a close friendship with both.

Upon returning from our honeymoon, I did report to the dispensary for work every day. But again, the Captain, a medical officer, was very thoughtful. He indicated that I needn't come in every day or even for a full day. Everyone knew that my time was limited in Berchtesgaden. I anticipated my travel orders for Toledo any day.

Ironically, after only twenty days after our wedding on August 25, 1947, Fran came to the dispensary very excited. She had her passport, visa, and travel orders to Toledo, Ohio. I was shocked. I was still waiting for my orders. Fran had a travel date from Berchtesgaden to Bremerhaven. At Bremerhaven, she was to report to the Army Dependent Housing Building until departure for the United States. I immediately contacted our Headquarters at Bad Tolz to advise them of the details of Fran's documents. They took action immediately to prepare my orders so that Fran and I would travel together. Yes, it paid to have friends along the way. In only a matter of days, I received my orders.

We were on our way to Toledo, Ohio, in late September, 1947. The trials and tribulations that Fran and I endured to marry were all behind us. Yes, it required both of us to be patient. I stayed one year longer in the Army. This was not too bad as the future proved. The extra year also provided me with twelve more months of college education under th G.I. Bill of Rights. Of course that was the last thing on my mind when I volunteered for one year. Needless to say, I was ready to sign for more years in the Army if the wedding ban was not lifted. No doubt the waiting period and all of the documentation required tested the resolve of many Americans wanting to marry German nationals. I always believed that any American who went through all of the trials and tribulations to marry a German and later determined it was a mistake would have to be an unusual person. I have no doubts that many such marriages did fail for various reasons.

In retrospect, both Frances and I believe that we were very fortunate. Having met and become serious in our relationship, I was fortunate to be in Army organizations that were relatively small where the men knew one another. While assigned to the 633rd Medical Clearing Company in Ludwigsburg, Germany, I was extremely blessed by having understanding superiors who gave me tremendous leeway in traveling to and from Berchtesgaden. They permitted me to have Army extensions as a draftee to my Army tour, and also providing me with sound advice on choosing alternatives for remaining in Germany until the Army lifted the wedding ban.

Frances and I were also fortunate in Bechtesgaden. Again, the medical unit I was assigned to was comprised of approximately ten Army personnel. We had outstanding American and German friends plus numerous acquaintances in Berchtesgaden who accommodated us with various favors prior to and particularly after our marriage. When we look back at those years and times, we know that we were Blessed during what appeared to be very challenging periods of our lives.

As of this year, 2005, our fifty seven plus years of togetherness attests to our love, dedication, and the Army making the correct decision to approve our marriage in 1947. We may not have been the first American/German couple to wed after the Army lifted the wedding ban between the American military personnel and German nationals on January 1, 1947, but we certainly were the first in Berchtesgaden and no doubt among the first in all of Germany.

Since that unusual period in American and German relations, I have no doubt that literally tens of thousands of American military service personnel have married German nationals since 1947 and that such couples and their descendants can be found living in every one of these great United States.

The wedding picture taken on August 25, 1947, at the front of the Stifts Church following the church ceremony.

A picture of Frances taken at the Bellevue Hotel at a small reception.

Epilogue

August 25, 1947, seems as though it was just few months ago. The years have passed too rapidly. Since that year, Fran and I have raised three boys. Each has grown into manhood. Two of our three sons, Robert and Gregory, were born in Mercy Hospital located in Toledo, Ohio. Robert and Gregory were born prior to my eight years of employment with the United States Army in Germany, two years in Bremerhaven and six years in Mannheim, that started in July, 1957.

The fact that I had signed a document in 1947 that I would never return to Germany was no longer applicable. History in the form of the "cold war" changed the American attitudes and the international political scene.

David, our third son, was born in an Army dispensary in the American military compound knows as "Benjamin Franklin Village" located just outside of Mannheim, Germany. David's birth was more dramatic than Robert's and Gregory's in Toledo. The Army ambulance transporting Frances to the American military hospital in Heidelberg, Germany, was stopped on the German autobahn just outside of Mannheim. Traffic was at a standstill. Fortunately, I was following the ambulance and directed the ambulance driver to return to the dispensary in the Village. Within minutes after arriving back at the dispensary David was born. He and Frances were transported by ambulance via the secondary roads to the American military hospital in Heidelberg, Germany.

All of the family have traveled from Alexandria, Virginia, to Toledo many times over the years visiting my siblings, nephews, nieces, and "old" friends. Fran and I have visited Berchtesgaden and other parts of Germany very often since 1965 after our return with the family to the United States and Virginia. We call Virginia home.

About The Author

Melvin R. Bielawski is a World War II veteran. After his induction into the Army, Mr. Bielawski received infantry training at Ft. McClellan, Alabama. Subsequent to his basic infantry training, he was ordered to Germany, in November, 1945, and was assigned to the 633rd Medical Clearing Company located in Ludwigsburg, Germany. He was given a medical MOS (military occupation specialty) and placed in charge of the hospital in the Prisoner of War (P.O.W.) Camp 78, in Zuffenhausen, Germany.

While on leave in Berchtesgaden, Germany, in July, 1946, he met his future wife, Frances, at Koenigsee a mountain lake in Bavaria. They were one of the first American/German couples to be married in Germany after General Eisenhower lifted the non-fraternization and wedding bans on January 1, 1947.

Following his military discharge in 1947, Mr. Bielawski attended the University of Toledo (UT) under the G.I. Bill of Rights. He majored in Industrial Management (BBA). While employed by the Department of Defense in the Washington area, he attended George Washington University and received his M.S. in Public and Government Administration. He retired from the Department of Defense in 1982. He and his wife reside in Alexandria, Virginia. He is currently active in writing both fiction and nonfiction, fishing, golf, and traveling with his wife, Frances.

He is the author of "The Corner", a documentary about his neighborhood in Toledo during the late 1930's, through WW II,

and the early 1950's. He has donated the publication rights to The Institute on World War II & the Human Experience, Florida State University. A copy of the documentary is also on file in the Lucas County/Toledo Main Library. His book, "Secession", a thrilling novel that deals with a special group of Americans who plot successfully to select one of the United States for secession from the nation, was recently published by 1st Books Library.

Printed in the United States
33380LVS00004B/128

9 781420 810936